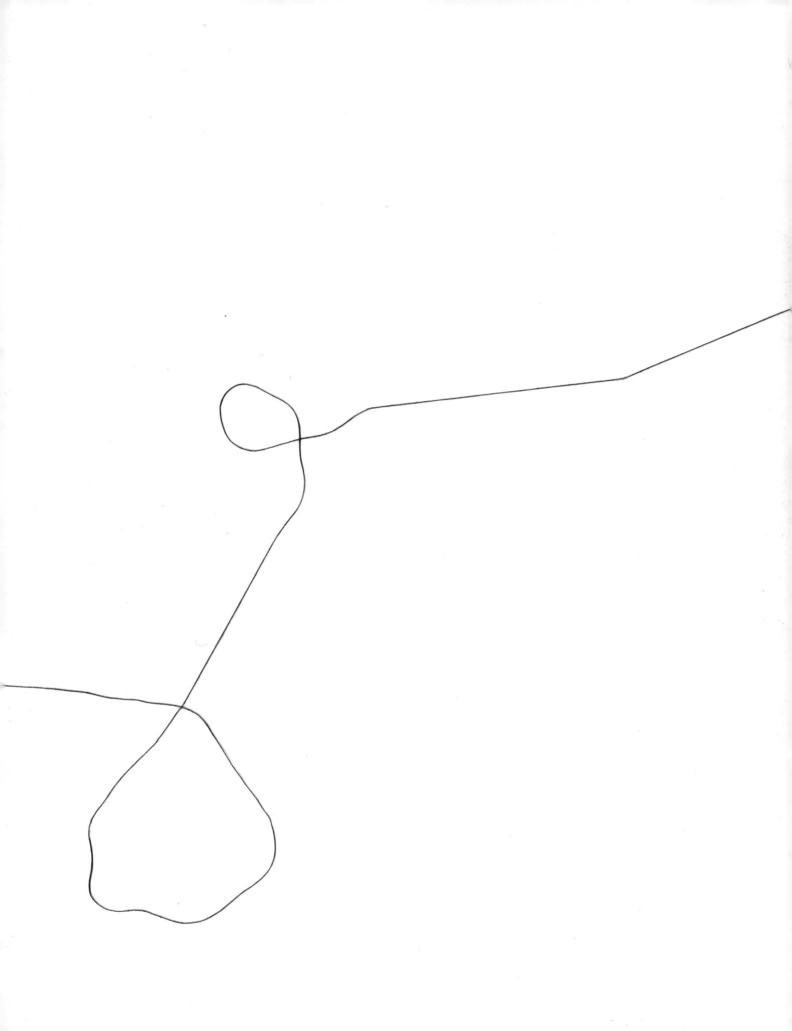

this book
belongs to:

First published in the United States of America in 2010 by
Rizzoli International Publications, Inc.
300 Park Avenue South
New York, NY 10010
Www.rizzoliusa.com

Designed by A/Z

Distributed to the U.S. Trade by Random House, New York

ISBN-13: 978-0-8478-3365-8
Library of Congress Control Number: 2010929449
Printed and bound in China
2010 2011 2012 2013 2014 / 10 9 8 7 6 5 4 3 2 1

a perfectly kept
house is the sign
of a misspent life.
MARY RANDOLPH CARTER

a perfectly kept house is the sign of a misspent life.

MARY RANDOLPH CARTER

How to live creatively with collections, clutter, work, kids, pets, art, etc... and stop worrying about everything being perfectly in its place.

Written and Photographed by
Mary Randolph Carter

RIZZOLI
NEW YORK

New York · Paris · London · Milan

dedication

For my mother,
who has always believed
a perfectly kept house
can't compare with
a home filled with living.

Contents

in the beginning

How I fell in love with lived-in, not perfectly kept, homes filled with collections, memories, children, pets, clutter, work, and lots of creativity.

At the worst, a house unkept cannot be so distressing as a life unlived.

Dame Rose Macaulay (1881-1958)

For many years the first thing to greet us on visits home, scuffed to near illegibility by the passage of time and the comings and goings of the nine of us—my six sisters and two brothers, plus husbands, wives, children, grandchildren, neighbors, and friends—was a muddied message on the doormat at the entrance to Muskettoe Pointe Farm. It was discovered one Christmas Eve on a panicky last-minute family shopping spree. Three of us spied a pile of them in the holiday rubble of one of those big discount stores. We all pounced and decided right then it was the perfect gift to give one another, plus one for our mother and father. "A perfectly kept house is the sign of a misspent life" became a family motto—and, ultimately, the title of this book.

We never really questioned who might have uttered such a piece of heartfelt wisdom, swiped by some clever marketer to live an ignominious life underfoot. But it may have been one Dame Rose Macaulay (1881–1958), who put it this way, "At the worst, a house unkept cannot be so distressing as a life unlived." My siblings and I were raised to live that way, which is why I think our friends enjoyed coming to our home. Our house was lived-in but not "unkept," as Dame Rose puts it. We all contributed to keeping the best order we could given the hubbub of a large, lively family. Floors were polished, silver wasn't. We preferred candlelight to lamplight, which created a mood of

Previous spread: A photograph of me proudly displaying a portrait of Elm Glen Farm, our home in upstate New York, painted by the former owner. Clockwise from top center: Thrift-shop paintings; the family doormat that became our motto; a caught moment of living with children; a child's silhouette; my father and mother; Dame Rose Macaulay's words; a pair of old mulberry trees in the field beyond our farmhouse in upstate New York; the welcome of candlelit windows.

comfort and hid a smudge or chip in our old plaster walls. We once pulled an old weathered picnic table into the kitchen to accommodate extra guests and then left it there. Though the main part of our house was built in the seventeenth century, and we drank our milk out of little pewter cups, the milk itself was self-served out of a stainless steel restaurant machine.

When people entered our home they became part of the family. They were invited to participate: to create a meal, set a table, light the candles, pour the wine, build a fire, make a toast, tell a story, wash the dishes, sing and dance, laugh out loud, celebrate—live! Pedro Guerrero, a photographer who made his living photographing quite perfect homes for magazines, recalls arriving at the residence of Alexander and Louisa Calder in Roxbury, Connecticut, in 1963. The first surprise was that their typical Connecticut farmhouse was painted black. The bigger shock was walking into their kitchen. It was unlike any room he had ever been assigned to document before and inspired his book, *Calder at Home*, in which he wrote, "it was a kitchen to be used, not to impress. It told me everything that I didn't already know about these people—their charm, their informality, their intense passion, a life lived without pretense or sham."

All through my life, thanks to images in books and magazines, I have tiptoed through homes like this that somehow felt akin to the one I grew up in. I have cut out some of my favorite images and collected them in scrap-

Clockwise from top left: An homage to dogs; a piece of family history; the Calder kitchen; a saved issue of The World of Interiors; *Alexander Calder's desk; a watercolor of heirloom spoons; a Fourth of July picnic served up on an old weathered table.*

THE WORLD OF
INTERIORS

JUNE 1989 $3.95

Alexander Calder in the creative clutter of his studio in Roxbury, Connecticut.

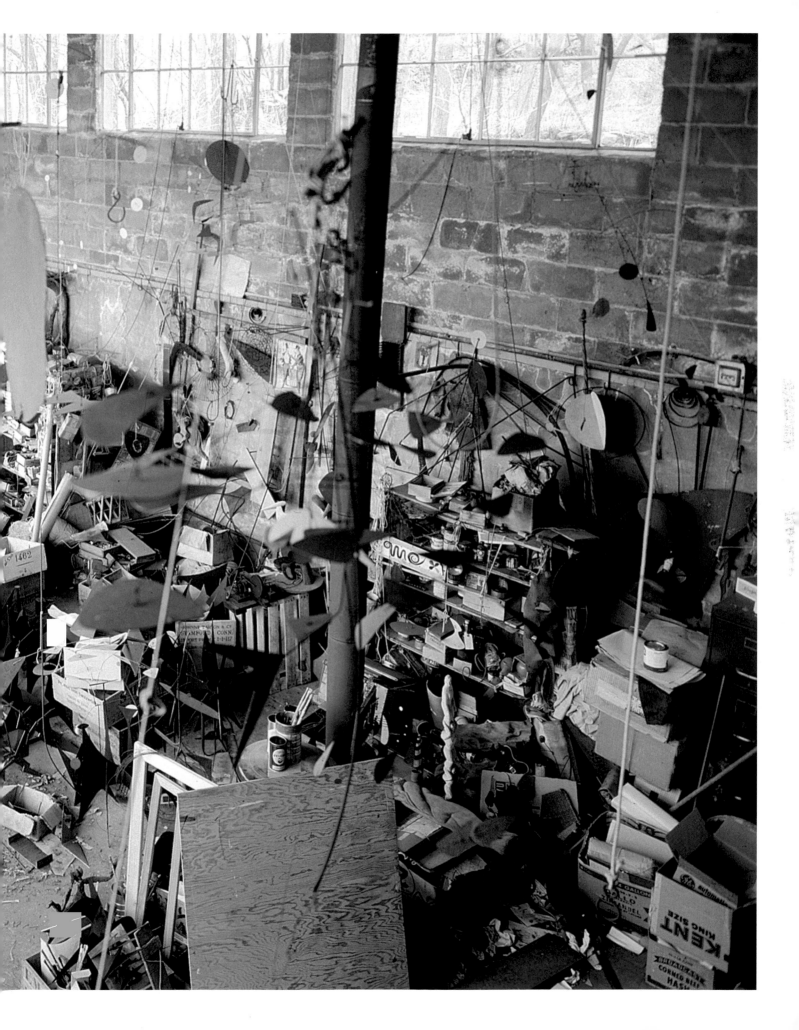

books, or kept the articles about the homes intact, feeling unworthy to pull them apart. I have marked them with scribbled-on scraps of paper or multicolored Post-its, so at any moment I can make a return visit to the enchanted ruin in Oxfordshire, England, lived in by Hugh and Beeban Morris and their pet crow and large family, both of which are archived in my collection of *World of Interiors*. I can knock on the door of Little Hyttnas, the handcrafted home of Karin and Carl Larsson and their seven children in the little Swedish village of Sundborn. I can wander again through Charleston Farmhouse, in Sussex, England, the gloriously imperfect refuge of Vanessa Bell, Duncan Grant, and their artistically disheveled friends and family that I documented in 1968. Or I can follow the lens of David Douglas Duncan into the inner sanctum of Picasso's La Villa California, and roam the living rooms of the master of creative clutter himself. All of these and more have inspired my feelings about what a home should be.

Less well known are the eight case histories documented in this book. Each one inspires and offers solutions for living with the things we love the most, and each substantiates in some way my own personal theories about the beauty of the imperfect life, including housekeeping, clutter, comfort, ambience, welcomes, the unmade bed, the purposeless room, an imperfect desk, hospitality, and informality. There are no rules. Just scuff the mud off your shoes on my old doormat, come in, and join the living.

Clockwise from top left: Charleston Farmhouse in the village of Firle, in Sussex, England; the studio at Charleston; a watercolor by Carl Larsson of his children at play; a scrapbook mantel in the Charleston studio; my imaginary ideal of me as a child; a Venetian chair in the Charleston library; taking a picture of the bust of Virginia Woolf, Charleston Farmhouse, 1986.

housekeeping

Liberated from old-fashioned roles,
we can now embrace our homes less
with the housekeeper's broom and
more with the homemaker's heart.

housekeeping is a term that seems a little old-fashioned today. And although we tend to associate it with cleaning, I prefer to embrace the term very literally—we are the keepers of our houses. If you live in something other than a house—an apartment, for example—you are still a housekeeper, never an apartment-keeper. In this context house stands for home, though in my mind they are very different things.

When I was growing up, the woman of the house was known as a housewife, responsible for cleaning the house, doing the laundry, shopping, cooking, and all those daily tasks that kept the house orderly and running smoothly. If you were a housewife who had children that meant you had dual roles—mother and housekeeper. I never thought of my mother as a housewife. It was a term that didn't seem to fit. She was a wife and a mother of nine children. She was always active—working, volunteering, and eventually the head of her own business. Our home was always perfect: it was comfortable and personal. My mother was very literally a homemaker.

My early womanhood was defined in part by the women's liberation movement, and a "housewife" was something my liberated friends and I never wanted to be. We wanted to be identified as workers who left the home and made our contribution in an environment that had to do with using our

brains, not our mops. What were we thinking? That we could do it all, of course, and in some ways we did. We got to go to work and clean, but not necessarily all alone. Most of us married men who appreciated that if we were going to help bring home the bacon, we needed help cooking it. Roles around housekeeping were definitely evolving. When children came, it was perfectly acceptable for women (if they had the economic option) to decline returning to work for full-time motherhood. For those of us who decided to work outside the home, figuring out childcare was a major issue.

Hiring someone to care for our children (and clean our houses) while we were pursuing our careers was not something most of our mothers had done. And not only were there issues to be solved between new mothers and new fathers about raising new children, but lots of potentially divisive issues between the women (housewives) who stayed home and those who didn't. These were, lest we forget, the pioneer days of a new order of womanhood, manhood, and housekeeping, and though the dust has hardly settled, I think it's safe to say things are a lot clearer; consciousness-raising groups are a thing of the past.

Though I still don't relish housekeeping, I have never felt defined by it. If we're fortunate enough, it is just one of the roles in a life full of options and experiences we can choose. When it's time to sweep the kitchen floor, wash the dishes, do the laundry, dust

away the cobwebs, make up the beds, or prepare a meal, we do it with a mostly positive kind of energy. I love my house. I am its keeper. I want it to be comfortable, not perfect. I want my family and friends to feel like they can curl up in a chair with a pile of magazines or books spread out around them. On the other hand, I don't believe in living in a mess. Order can be liberating as long as it's not artificial or rigid, turning a perfectly beautiful house into an untouchable ice palace. Geri Roper (Case History No. 5, page 133) thinks people love her house because "it's lived-in." For me, this is what good housekeeping is all about: keeping our houses real and making them places that embrace everyday living, not just showy houses for company. Housekeeping is about transforming our domicile into a home. As homemakers it's what we strive for, though sometimes unconsciously. I don't think a child sets out to make his or her bedroom or private corner into a home. But when he places his favorite blanket or doll or bear on his pillow, he has marked the place as his home. The bed is no longer just a bed. When we hang a brass knocker, nameplate, or wreath on the front door of our house or apartment, we declare: This is my home. Over time that house becomes a home by the simple act of living in it with the things and people and animals that we love.

> ## "I want my house to be comfortable, not perfect."
> —Carter

Previous spread: Stand firm on your own principles of housekeeping, down to how often you shake the dust out of a favorite rag rug.
Opposite: Two "home" makers—my mother and me.
Left: A lived-in chair in my home.

23

coming clean

It's great to have an excuse for not cleaning your house. Writing a book is one of the best. How many times do I tell myself it's more important for me to write than to vacuum the living room rug? My answer: many times. But there are times, like the day I was writing this chapter, when that excuse would not work. My son and his girlfriend were coming for dinner. She (being a new girlfriend) had never been to our house, and I, desiring to make it feel like the welcoming home my son is proud of, needed to do which? A. Write another chapter on my imperfect house; B. Surrender the computer for the vacuum cleaner, the Swiffer, and a dust cloth. What to do?

In researching the case histories for this book, one of the most revealing of the forty-seven housekeeping questions I asked was, "Do you clean for yourself or for company?" And though the answers were all rather different, as were the circumstances, all participants agreed that cleaning is a necessary evil. My own motivations vary: company is a major one; the home wedding of our older son was a huge one; and Thanksgiving dinner is definitely one of my top five reasons to clean. But do I clean for myself? I'd have to say, rarely, except for things that really bug me like a dirty kitchen floor, dishes in the sink, a vase of dead flowers, sofa pillows askew, and toothpaste dribbles in the sink. What can be postponed indefinitely? Washing windows and cleaning out the attic, the basement, the barn, the bottom of my closet, the bathroom cabinet under the sink, our overburdened hall closet, and our sons' baseball card collection

tucked up into the upper reaches of their old closet. Most of this task-laden litany, except perhaps the first—window-washing—falls less into the cleaning category, which is more about immediacy, the daily and weekly goals that keep our heads above water, and more into "Big Organizational Projects" to be tackled over time, requiring great focus and fortitude.

For me, the drag of cleaning up dates back to those annoying jobs scrawled under my name on the summer to-do list of my childhood. We never went away to camp because, given our number, nine of us plus visiting cousins and neighborhood friends, we were a camp. The anchor of those days was that big handmade posterboard list outlining all the day's duties and activities from dawn to dusk. We campers had to earn our fun—arts and crafts, swimming, singing, and lunch—by checking off our individual labors. Among them were the inglorious rituals of making our beds, washing our dishes, sweeping the kitchen floor, folding laundry, sorting socks in the family sock bag (worse than taking out the garbage), and feeding our household pets. Depending upon the year, this included two Siamese cats, two Saint Bernards, with and without litters of puppies, my parakeet Ernie, our pony Blue Tail, and our old horse Scrabble. I carry that old handwritten to-do list in my head, and with my siblings passed it on to our children during the summer camps we later improvised for them.

Answer to the multiple choice question?
B.

Housekeeping essentials at rest: a well-used broom, a copper vessel to collect the trash, a galvanized bucket to hold the kindling, a fireplace shovel to toss the ashes.

Is Cleanliness Next to Godliness?

This thought may have had its roots in ancient Hebrew writings. It was brought to light centuries later in a 1605 treatise by Francis Bacon, but it was John Wesley, the Anglican clergyman and cofounder of Methodism, who framed it as the proverb we know today, proclaiming from his pulpit in 1791, "Slovenliness is no part of religion. Cleanliness is indeed next to Godliness."

Taking the Old Testament view off the table, picture this proverb as a modern-day slogan. In other words, you're driving down the highway and on the bumper of the car in front of you is plastered a red and black bumper sticker that declares: Cleanliness is next to Godliness! Well, is it? I checked in with a few of my case history subjects, and two out of three responded with a resounding "No"; another accepted the notion but with some misgivings. Her feeling, like mine, is let's not sacrifice everything for a clean house.

Extending my own personal poll to the internet I came upon a family values Web site debating this very topic. One of my favorite points of view was expressed by a virtuous woman who wrote, "While I don't imagine that we honor God when our homes are in a state of disarray or chaos, I do believe that we can allow the pendulum to swing the other way and concentrate too much on housekeeping and not enough on things that matter." Those things are, of course, the family, friends, and animals that we love, which can be inconvenient and messy but should always override spotlessness. And come to think of it, as another friend who I pulled into this argument suggested, "Isn't God about love?"

A clean house is probably a little more godly than an unkempt house, which may account for the expression, "What an ungodly mess!" But a house that is scrubbed to death is at risk of something more ungodly—losing its soul.

Endurance Training

Some tips from our sort-of resident clean team, on getting clean or just enduring it!

- **One Step at a Time**
"I absolutely hate cleaning. I like cleaning little corners. It makes a huge difference, but the idea of doing it again is just too much."
—Natalie Gibson (Case History No. 7, page 189)

- **Mind Over Matter**
"Everything is routine in housekeeping, so I try to flavor my everyday tasks with good thoughts, so as not to drown in it or waste away my life."—Elena Salgueiro (Case History No. 4, page 105)

- **Never Go to Bed with Dirty Dishes**
"It annoys me to go to bed with dirty dishes, no matter how tired I am. When I wake up in the morning I want everything clean so I can boil the water and make my coffee and read the paper."—Oberto Gili (Case History No. 1, page 31)
"I could never go to sleep with a dirty cup in the sink just the way I couldn't sleep in the shirt I've worn all day. But, I could wear a shirt that's not ironed, just the way I could

sleep on unpressed sheets."—Pamela Bell (Case History No. 3, page 77)

❧ Create a Schedule
"I do my big cleaning on Mondays, after the weekend's possible skiddings (guests, feasts, and other let-it-go things). Tuesdays I do my shopping. Fridays I do a cosmetic rapid vacuuming."—Elena Salgueiro

❧ Start with What You Hate the Most
"I hate to wash the kitchen floor, but once it's done, it looks so good, I have the courage to move on!"—Elena Salgueiro

❧ Pick a Task to Do in Installments
"I can't get my dusting done in a day so I spread it out over the week. Don't forget to dust your plants!"—Elena Salgueiro

❧ Talk to Your Furniture . . . Reminisce
"There are times when I love to clean the house—a combination of the nesting instinct and a little of that 'talking to your plants' thing. Sometimes while dusting a piece, I will reminisce about where I found it, an encounter with a shopkeeper, or an excursion with a sister, friend, or child. At times you may think you're crazy to own all these things or else brilliant for finding these treasures so many other eyes missed!"—Liza Carter Norton (Case History No. 6, page 161)

❧ Don't Let the Dust and Dog Hair Get You Down! Give Yourself Some Credit for Other Things You Do Well
"Because of the four dogs I vacuum a lot, but

I probably don't dust as often as I should. I am certainly not a housekeeper, but I am a good homemaker. I'm really good at making a house warm. I can make any space feel welcoming."—Geri Roper (Case History no. 5, page 133)

The Writing's On the Wall
Leave it to my mother, the queen of common sense, to come up with the perfect solution for keeping track of phone numbers. (Keep in mind this was back in the pre-cell-phone era before she could program each of us by number—one to nine—as she has today.) It was around 1987 when she threw out the book (her telephone book that was always lost and always changing) and started penciling in names and phone numbers right on the wall above the phone next to her bed. Some people were a little shocked, especially children brought up not to scribble on the walls, but those of us who shared the problem applauded her audacity and practicality. Write on, Mom!

A perfect example of doing what works, not what's expected: my mother's bedside wall of scribbled phone numbers.

Open Windows

"Keep passing the open window,"* was the way my sister Christian and I would often close our letters to each other. It was a quote we both loved from John Irving's *The Hotel New Hampshire*. In its original context, it had a dark but slightly optimistic message to it, something like pass that open window, don't jump! We used it in a lighter way, but it brings to mind the inescapable fact that a lot of people today, particularly people who live and work in urban environments, live with windows that don't open.

For me, one of the simplest pleasures of life is opening a window. First there is the welcome air—warm or cold, humid, damp or frosty—moving against your face, hands, and body. Then there are the sounds that connect you instantly to life outside: the cacophony of nature in the country or city traffic—birds, frogs, and crickets, or the human interaction of children and their parents or friends walking and talking, yelling, laughing, or whistling. The howling of coyotes as they run wild in the country or the barking of dogs in the city. Seeing a sheer curtain float above a windowsill as a summer breeze whispers through tempts us to stop what we're doing and stand in its path.

* The exact quote came from the last sentence in John Irving's *The Hotel New Hampshire*, published in 1981: "Coach Bob knew it all along, you've got to get obsessed and stay obsessed. You have to keep passing the open windows."

The most romantic bed in the world lies beneath an open window, where fresh breezes stir a sheer curtain and cool the lucky person who will lay his or her head on the awaiting pillow.

living with work

A photographer who confesses he would sometimes rather live in a hotel nevertheless manages to make his home/studio welcoming and personal with room for work, cooking, and entertaining.

31

Oberto

Born in: Northern Italy
Family: four dogs, a cow, one ox, one bull, and four donkeys (in Italy)
Home: New York City
Lived there: fifteen years
Description: the ground and first floors of a turn-of-the-century New York brownstone cum garden in Greenwich Village
Challenges: to make a home away from his other home in Italy that also works as an office, and to live with all the mementos he has collected
Solutions: to hide nothing away from either clients or guests, and to do as little cleaning as possible
Inspiration: through interior-design photography, he has seen tons of ways of living, experiencing different tastes
Dream house: a hotel room with zero responsibility

Previous spread: Stacks of yellow photo boxes mingle with a stack of favorite books, an outdoor light fixture, and a wall of simply framed black-and-white images.

This page (clockwise from top): Time out for the busy photographer; an eclectic convention of mementos, seen again on page 39; a stack of photo journals rests in a garden chair.

Opposite: Though Oberto would never attempt to cover the beautiful old floors of his house, the tops of his tables are another thing entirely. This one from Bra is set with a tilty gold chandelier, a vase from Peru, a Quimper platter from France, and two Richard Avedon volumes. The pair of café chairs were rescued from a New York City junk shop.

Photographer Oberto Gili has a meeting in his home. But he's not cleaning up. Everything is laid out on one of the five big tables he's constantly bending over for work, for cooking, for entertaining, and for rearranging the mementos of his life. A photographer who travels around the world, he has two homes. The one on the ground and first floors of a brownstone in downtown New York City is not the home of his four dogs Racchetta, Pepina, Teseo, and Nerone; Violetta his cow; Bartolomeo the bull; an ox named Sergio; and the four donkeys Giulia, GiovePluto, Cleto, and Simone. They live at Il Picot, his farm in Bra, a village in Northern Italy, right near the home of his mother and brothers and lots of nieces and nephews. Though the two settings are different and New York sadly lacks his pets and the farm animals and gardens that supply his own flowers, fruits, vegetables, eggs, butter, and cheese, he sees them as the same. "When I'm in Italy," he says, "I want to be reminded of New York, and when I'm here I want to be reminded of Italy."

Another big difference is the sight of ubiquitous yellow photo boxes overflowing from the open shelves of his big office upstairs. New York is more the home of his work, and a place for meetings with clients, agents, magazine editors, and occasionally a lineup of models. Tomorrow's meeting is with a writer who will peruse the photographs he has neatly arranged on a table near the kitchen. They will not be hidden away from guests coming later for dinner. These friends will dine on another table in the kitchen area, and they are free to inspect these piles of pictures which, until the meeting tomorrow, are just another piece of Oberto's personal history on display throughout his home.

Nothing is off-limits in Oberto's world except the sacrosanct cherry desk made by his favorite carpenter in Bra, and his computer table in an adjoining room. Friends needn't ask permission to climb the stairs to his work atelier or to plunk down for a rest on the inviting sleigh bed there—a place for summer snoozes and overnight guests. And though these upper rooms are more the official work space of his home they are just as personal.

"My home is a mix of mementos of things that I got in places that I enjoyed and want to remember." And when he moved in with all of them some fifteen years ago, he found a place for everything. He divided the long, wide-open ground-floor room into a series of tableaux bookended by a front and back garden. It is the sunny back garden end of this room where he really lives. Here is where the kitchen can be found, along with his favorite marble-topped table customized for pasta and bread-making; the hated TV, which he admits is essential but is hidden inside a heavy wooden cabinet from a junk store in Italy; a comfortable red sofa that he never sits on but that provides a place for important friends—a Mao throw pillow and two old and new sock dolls; and, most important of all, the light streaming through the sliding glass doors to the garden.

Opposite: Though the cherry wood desk made by his favorite carpenter in Bra may appear "unorderly and unorganized," Oberto insists that it's not. Over the mantelpiece, cluttered with a Stubbs print of a leopard and assorted snapshots, swims a school of artful fish from St. Barts. To the left of the fish floats a metal "O. G.," his adopted logo.
Left: One of Oberto's photo diaries filled with boarding passes and Polaroids of his shoots and travels.

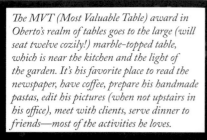

The MVT (Most Valuable Table) award in Oberto's realm of tables goes to the large (will seat twelve cozily!) marble-topped table, which is near the kitchen and the light of the garden. It's his favorite place to read the newspaper, have coffee, prepare his handmade pastas, edit his pictures (when not upstairs in his office), meet with clients, serve dinner to friends—most of the activities he loves.

This page (clockwise from top right):
A Moroccan lantern hangs from the kitchen beams; a platter of shells collected from beach shoots around the world; the essential TV and music system hidden in a painted cupboard—now you see it, now you don't.
Opposite: A painting of a young Mexican woman keeps watch over another table exhibit of Oberto mementos (seen up close on page 32) under the spotlight of a more modern chrome desk lamp.

Oberto loves tables, which is evident in this view of his totally open ground-floor living area. The table in the foreground serves as a perfect set for a man who has made his living capturing the details of other people's interiors. In the spirit of the burnished red Buddha candle in the center, there is a serenity to the way each object is placed—the pewter pitcher of blush roses, the plate of delicate shells gathered from beaches around the world, mismatched candlesticks, a primitive clay platter, and a pair of well-worn books.

The farther you move from this area the less lived-in the home feels, but this is the particular perspective of the man who has arranged every piece, including the cozy sofa at the far end of the room. "I hate couches. It is our bourgeoisie upbringing that makes us feel obligated to have a couch in the house." It is a concession he makes for guests who are grateful to find their way to it after a filling dinner of his homemade risotto. And though he understands the hygienic case for cleaning, he hates everything about it, mostly the sound of the vacuum cleaner. And what upsets him most is the way his still lifes get rearranged. He tries to do a little cleaning up when company is coming, but if he can't get to it, well, a little mess isn't so terrible. "If someone comes to my house it's because he or she truly likes people, and I try to make my home as friendly as possible." And that he does by allowing friends to share his life whether at work or at play, perfect or imperfect.

"My home is a mix of mementos…

that I got in places I enjoyed

and want to remember."

—Oberto

Opposite: Leave it to a photographer to come up with a quick fix for a dark corner. To add a little more light to this corner of his living room, Oberto just clipped a little utility light to the wing of an early American chair.
Top: A pillow portrait of Mao sits in an old painted green chair.
Bottom: The sleigh bed from Italy tucked into Oberto's large windowed office is a place for a snooze or overnight guests. The red egg-shaped lamp is from Hong Kong.

43

The Positive Side of a Messy Desk

Oberto has two desks in his semi–home office. The one seen at right, with his scanner and laptop computer, is free of the more tangible signs of work seen on his workhorse table on pages 36–37.

Sorting through a stack of papers in my office, I came across an article left there over a year ago by a colleague who knows me well. Copied out of *Time* magazine, it was titled "Messy Is the New Neat," by Jeremy Caplan. The irony hit me when I read the first sentence: "Neatness is overrated. Let those stacks of papers pile up on your desk." The article illuminates a theory espoused by the author of what was then a new book called *A Perfect Mess: the Hidden Benefits of Disorder* (Little, Brown). It was written by Columbia University professor Eric Abrahamson, who described himself as a "scholar of organization behavior" and who admits to being a bit of a mess. It goes on to advise neatniks, in particular, that what they hold as virtuous may in fact be wasted time. Filing things out of sight often prevents their usefulness. Perfect examples: my fateful discovery of the article made accessible by my own haphazard filing system, and the very useful, everything-in-the-open shelving system of the anti-neatnik photographer Oberto Gili.

Oberto's work-at-home haven and heaven: a sunny office with a view of the garden, lots of storage for archiving old prints, and an oversized farmhouse table for the not-so-rustic computer that is flanked by a stately pair of vintage lamps.

clutter

Finding solace and a little beauty in
the clutter of the things we cherish
in our everyday lives at home and
at work.

here is mess and there is clutter. If you grew up with the former—for example, you shared a room with a brother or sister whose belongings (toys, clothes, books, sporting equipment, records, games) were spread out like a minefield all over your room—you probably make no distinction. Clutter vigilantes contend that clutter is always a mess; clutter connoisseurs contend that clutter is liberation from the rigidity of over-organization.

Elena Salgueiro (Case History No. 4, page 105), mother of five and helpless lover of junk, defines clutter as "a skillfully arranged state of spirit," whereas mess for her is "a disarranged mind." "Clutter," she continues, "is all the things you most need, never use, but can't part with." These are the things that fall outside of the necessities of life but sustain the collector's heart and soul. "The house is cluttered when it is too small to contain the whole of your dreams," Elena contends, but then relents, "I know I would clutter the biggest house I could get my hands on as well."

A cluttered house is a lived-in house. It is filled with signs of life: stacks of magazines; newspapers spread over a sofa; books piled next to the bed; a desk arranged with letters, invitations, and family photos; children's artwork tacked to the wall or displayed on the refrigerator. Clutter speaks to activity. A book started, a painting begun, children's books opened on the kitchen table, a teacup next to a piece of chocolate cake. Everything

in its place may give a certain satisfaction, but a lived-in room exudes comfort and warmth. We sit on a sofa, we push a pillow underneath our head, we pull a soft blanket around us, and we settle down for a little nap. When we get up to leave, the signs of our living remain— cushions slightly askew, a coverlet falling off the sofa, the open pages of an old leather journal, a pair of sneakers lost under the sofa. Clutter is life lived out in the open. Things aren't hidden away but shared. Rooms that have real character are apt to be embellished with books, paintings, wooden boxes, bowls of fruit, pillows, and collections of things that have meaning to the people who live there. Rooms want to feel lived-in, and clutter— accessories, mementos, collections, call it what you like—adds that unique character.

Pamela Bell (Case History No. 3, page 77) treats the clutter in her life with more restraint. The old suitcases she collects are stacked neatly in a living room corner topped off with another stack of well-loved books. The personal touches on her bedroom writing table—a Batman Pez dispenser, a swirly glass paperweight, her son Will's ceramic project, a scented candle, a small crock of flowers, and two more jars filled with writing instruments—are thoughtfully arranged so that each has a kind of prominence. It is the same with the floor-to-ceiling scrapbook wall that frames the colorful originality of her children's artwork. Her love of each hand-drawn piece and "mommy" message is conveyed in its careful thumbtacked symmetry. An adjacent wall anchored by a large flat-screen TV surrounded

by her personal collection of photography and artwork is composed quite similarly. "I take nothing that my children do for granted," she says. Will's red, white, and blue shield with the star in the center is exhibited on a contemporary glass desk next to a decoupage mask done by her daughter Anabel. They're just as important to her as the large photograph hanging near them created by a well-known artist whose work has also been exhibited at the Whitney Museum.

Oberto Gili's clutter (Case History No. 1, page 31) is made up of the mementos he has gathered from shooting pictures around the world. "They are very important to me because everything is a recollection. Mostly I got them because of what they tell me not because of their value. I don't care if they are great pieces or junk." A perfect example is the miniature entourage circling the pedestal dish of tangerines in the center of his marble-topped kitchen table (pages 36–37). They include a Chinese flag stuck in a conch shell, a brass replica of the Eiffel Tower, a doll-sized porcelain tea set, a pair of white and black dogs given to him by a stylist friend, a pair of grasshoppers from China, a tiny emperor of Russia, and an old glass bottle encrusted with ceramic flowers. On the next table

"Clutter is a grand parade that follows us all our days from a playpen of toys…to the places we call home."

Previous spread: A wall cluttered with images that personally appeal to us makes a blank surface a canvas of our imaginations.
Opposite: Charming mementos of Oberto Gili's friends and travels surround a pedestal of oranges on a marble-topped table.
Left: Old suitcases remind Pamela Bell of the mystery of travel. Stacked up in her living room, they support another passion—photography books.

(seen on pages 40–41) there is a red Buddha candle surrounded by a posse of perfect white conch shells, mismatched candlesticks, antique books, pale pink roses, and a plate of the shells he has picked up from beaches all over the world. It is a still life of souvenirs from his own life, but not unlike the many he has discovered in the hundreds of personal domains he has documented for magazines and in his own books for over three decades. He sets them up and moves them around, but he never throws anything away.

Clutter is the poetry of our homes. It is a fingerprint of an experience, a souvenir of our childhoods, an expression of our humor, a collection of things that we just can't live without. Clutter gives life to ordinary things—a mantelpiece decorated with a lone pair of candlesticks becomes standing-room-only to transient invitations, postcards, snapshots, children's artwork, and errant bric-a-brac; undistinguished shelves of books make room for character-building photographs, paintings, and personal objects; a blank wall becomes a patchwork of pictures; an old trunk top is warmed up with a stack of colorful coverlets; a plain windowsill gets cozy lined with a frieze of wooden toys mixed with fragrant pots of herbs. Clutter is a grand parade that follows us all our days, from a playpen filled with toys to the scrapbooklike walls of our college dorms, our first work cubicles, our first apartments, and the places we call home. Embrace it, make peace with it, take control of it, share it, reorganize it, and when the time seems right, bid it farewell.

Opposite: A corner bookshelf is embellished with the personal touch of a child's handmade calendar, a picture of Saint Theresa, a pink plaid doll's trunk, and giant wooden rosary beads. Closing in on it is the artful clutter of Paint-by-Number and thrift-shop paintings.
This page: Floating fish decoys and a buoy.

51

Artistic clutter poetically strewn throughout a log cabin atelier includes tacked and perched paintings; haphazardly piled books; a roll of watercolors tied with ribbon and sketchbooks resting on an ottoman; an unfinished book dropped momentarily on a floor cushion; and the wrinkles of a paisley shawl romancing the rustic four-poster log bed.

clutter at work

A Perfectly Kept Office Is the Sign of a Misspent Life

There is a scene in *Karl Lagerfeld Confidential*, a French documentary about the designer's life, when he is sitting quietly sketching at a table surrounded by mountains of books and creative disturbance. In a rare moment we catch him without his dark glasses, but other than that he is perfectly groomed with his white hair pulled back in a neat little peruke, garbed in his usual clerical-like collar and priestly black garments. He is sketching a tulle dress that may or may not walk down a real runway. He is quite quiet. All of a sudden he speaks and his words are a shock, subtitled in English on the screen: "I am persnickety. But I like disorder when I am at work. I would freeze at a tidy desk."

Artistic Clutter

Many people prefer disorder around them when they work. Though they may be perfectly orderly in their personal appearance and in the way they appoint their homes, the opposite is preferred when they are working. It seems quite typical that the artist's studio be a bit of a hodgepodge. There are so many accessories involved in what they do—canvases, paints, brushes, stretchers, sets, and still lifes. Picasso was the master of creative clutter. He was inspired to work and live that way. Alexander Calder could have been his American brother. His first studio in Roxbury, Connecticut, was a tangle of coiled wire, hammers, snips, and drills. Photographer Pedro Guerrero caught "Sandy," as Calder was called, in the midst of all of this in his cinder-block studio in Roxbury in the early sixties (pages 16–17). Guerrero writes in his book, *Calder at Home*, that Sandy made it clear to him that what seemed to be clutter was in fact highly organized chaos.

In Case History No. 8 (on page 219), Daniela Kamiliotis, an artist like Calder with a studio in another part of Connecticut, would concur. Though her creative tools are those of a painter, potter, and designer of women's fashion, she thrives in a crowded workspace that evokes romance and fantasy. "Since both my parents were actors and my first career in my native Romania was designing costumes for the theater, I always set up my studio like a kind of stage set inspired by and inspiring whatever it is I am dreaming of." Nathalie Lété, Case History No. 2 (page 61), another artist, whose studio outside of Paris was once the birthplace of some of the actual girders of the Eiffel Tower, feels quite differently about her cluttered atelier. "All the mess is very disturbing, particularly when I am starting a new project." But feeling helpless against the limits of time—not enough of it to spare to organize the overflow of the multiple projects she is constantly working on, from paintings to sewing, books, ceramics, even huge illustrated carpets—clutter piles up around her like a beautiful prison. Her dream is to return it to the way it was when she moved in eight years ago, "quite clear and empty, very beautiful and organized." She feels she would thrive in a more Zen-like workspace, but for now that seems out of the question. Though she has found ways to navigate through the offspring of her creativity, like committing different activities and projects to different worktables, her original vision was a more flexible space

Karl Lagerfeld and I have something in common: we love to work surrounded by personal clutter. Mine (at home) includes family photographs, postcards, and drawings; thrift-shop paintings; hand-carved animals; and, to hide the underground headquarters of my printer and scanner, a makeshift desk skirt of my teenage rock 'n' roll hero, Elvis!

where things could be moved around. Now all her furnishings and worktables are so laden with layers of work they won't move an inch!

Home Work

I always marvel at people who are able to live and work in the same place. It requires great discipline to organize the time and space for both activities, and tremendous focus to prevent the distractions of home—personal accessories, chores, children, and pets—from interfering. Perhaps because his nomadic craft keeps him away from home so often, Oberto Gili, our photographer in Case History No. 1 (page 31), would have it no other way. He has no problem turning the marble-topped table he rolls out his homemade pasta on into a conference table for meetings with clients. And though he has designated two upstairs rooms as office space with worktables, counters, computers, and storage for endless boxes of contact sheets and prints, he can just as easily make room in them (thanks to a large daybed seen on page 43) for overnight guests. And those guests seem happy, even privileged, to spend the night surrounded by the creative detritus of their generous host. It is the same with my son Carter Berg, who has carved out a nice slice of the New York City apartment living room he shares with his wife Kasia into a home office for himself. When guests arrive for the evening, the compromise is to clear off his two worktables and put them to a different kind of work—serving dinner.

The Comfort of Clutter

I have always worked in the comfort of personal clutter both at home and at work. I am happiest surrounded in either place by stacks of books, magazines, tear sheets, photographs, contact sheets, jars of Sharpie markers, pencils, wooden rulers, old alarm clocks, postcards, letters, magnifying glasses, and ubiquitous Post-it pads in pink, yellow, blue, and lime green. My jobs have always positioned me in the vortex (make that dust storm!) of creative frenzy. When colleagues pass by my office door showing around family members, guests, or new employees, I hear them whisper, "Oh, this is Carter's office—she's creative," as if that is the best excuse they can offer for what lies inside. For almost half of my working life that doorway looked into a large corner office overlooking Madison Avenue. By the time I moved out of it a year ago, the Collyer brothers would have been proud of my accumulated treasures. Each of the seven windowsills was stacked high with precarious piles of books, and on top of them toy trucks, a pair of children's frog boots, a handmade boat model, a vintage box of O.K. washing powder—all kinds of souvenirs from the photo shoots I have overseen for so many years. My avocation has definitely fed my junker's streak and vice-versa.

When I first moved into this space seventeen years ago, it was bare-bones cozy, furnished minimally with an old rolltop desk, a prop from one of my first photo shoots for Ralph Lauren, an eight-foot-long country worktable, a weathered blue step-back cupboard to hold my light box for editing chromes (now practically obsolete), painted shutters, benches (extra storage for books, not seating) and scattered Navajo rugs on the raw cement floor that I had requested instead of wall-to-wall carpeting. On my first day, as a welcome

gift, there was an apple tree blooming in the corner. When the leaves fell and didn't return I replaced it with another—a Ficus tree, a variety I had had some luck with in our apartment. When it failed, I gave up, until one day at a shoot on Long Island, one of my good and resourceful associates came up the beach dragging behind him a driftwood tree. For seventeen years its scrawny, desiccated branches thrived with mementos contributed by members of my team. It became the "scrapbook tree" of the department, sharing a collective personality and in a very singular way keeping everything organized.

I am never distracted by the excess of my office; in fact, its color and texture have always been an inspiring backdrop for me during the long hours I spend in it—my home away from home. I know where everything is, which is astonishing to all but those who choose to work similarly. A former office neighbor, whose door lined up a foot away from mine, was the Yin to my Yang. Her office was totally spare—not a loose paper or pile in sight. She would often drop by and marvel at my office style, and I at hers. Neither of us yearned for what the other had or hadn't, but appreciated each other's individual work environments and the systems that supported our nine-to-five lives.

What works for you in a given time or place—be it workplace or home—is the perfect way for you, but not necessarily the way for your neighbor, your best friend, or even your spouse. Here are a few tips from those who have seen the light at the end of the clutter!

Opposite: Little filing drawers in my old rolltop desk support tiny images and minature souvenirs.
Left: A screen of weathered shutters next to my real office desk offers privacy from a door on the other side and a place to tack up myriad inspirations.

Clutter-Up: Tips

● Don't let the overflow from one project run into another. Finish one, clean it up, and put it away. Or, if you're working on multiple projects at once, color code them with different colored files or Post-its.

● Try to use different work surfaces to lay out your stuff. When you run out of surfaces, use the floor.

● Try to clean up or at least neaten up your primary work area before you leave for the day.

● Learn to do as much as possible on your computer, unlike me who physically lays everything all over.

● Don't let your inspiration overwhelm the job at hand.

● Keep articles, e-mails, and images that have inspired you close at hand in a folder or in-box marked "random inspiration." Make a habit of revisiting it every month or six weeks. You may turn up an idea that is totally relevant to something you're working on now (see "The Positive Side of a Messy Desk," page 44) and toss things that are no longer inspiring or totally out of date.

● Obviously, there are limits to how far you can personalize your workspace, particularly if you work in a more corporate environment, but even the President of the United States has pictures of his family around him and memorabilia that keep him in touch with his personal self.

To make my office feel more homey, I've used the counter of an old painted cupboard as a spot for my light box and the back wall for saving memories of my career journey. The shelves above hold souvenirs from photo shoots, including, at top left, a nest I carried back from Ireland.

living with bric-a-brac

case history no. 2 **nathalie lété**

An artist living with her family in a converted factory outside Paris carves out a private space in which she can freely create a prodigious number of paintings, books, textiles, ceramics, and toys.

nathalie

Born in: Paris
Family: her husband Thomas Fougeirol,
and their children Angéle, 15, and
Oskar, 12
Home: Ivry, Paris
Lived there: eight years
Description: converted factory that once
made girders for the Eiffel Tower
Challenge: to create a home for her family
and a separate home for her work,
without distancing herself from either
Solution: finding a place to live that
offers both
Inspiration: Little Red Riding Hood, old
toys, and the birds and happy animals
of the forest
Words to live by: to feel really free
Dream: to have a pristine studio with
nothing but white walls and a long table

*Previous spread: Nathalie's Eiffel
Tower box of puzzles.*
*This page (clockwise from top): The
artist at work in her studio; a hand-
painted ceramic head of Nathalie's
Little Red Riding Hood; a natural
green tunnel to Nathalie's atelier.*
*Opposite: In front of her wall of naive
paintings created on wood, cardboard,
and even glass, a chorus line of Nathalie's look-alikes—her one-of-a-kind
hand-painted Red Riding Hood
ceramics—hobnob with other works
of art including her hand-tufted
"Patch" rug.*

ittle Red Riding Hood lives here. Though her real name is Nathalie Lété, which is a French translation of the one bequeathed by her German mother and Chinese father, it is her likeness that I see over and over again on the faces of a lineup of ceramic Little Red Riding Hoods as I peer into a large glass window of her atelier in Ivry, on the outskirts of Paris. What I see is what I saw as a child looking through the magic window of our clunky old TV—an idealized playroom created for the children's show *Romper Room*. That fantasy set had everything: perfect little wooden worktables and chairs; buckets of crayons, drawing pencils, and paintbrushes; finger paints; watercolor trays; stacks of colorful construction paper; pots of white paste; mounds of red, blue, green, and yellow modeling clay; candy-colored plastic scissors; stacks of games; shelves filled with every storybook you ever wanted to read; bins of building blocks; shelves of toys and every kind of stuffed animal and doll. Nathalie's atelier on the ground floor of what had been an industrial factory whose early claim to fame was creating the hefty girders of the Eiffel Tower, now offers airy work/live-in lofts for about sixty families, many of them artists like her and husband Thomas Fougeirol. His studio, right above hers, is reached by an outside metal stairway. In warm weather it is entwined with thick vines of wisteria, which soften the look but not the sound of the clanging footsteps of an approaching visitor. Filled with oversized canvases and painter's tools, it is more the ar-

tistic scene one would expect, but Nathalie's, down below, is the adult-sized realization of my childhood *Romper Room*. It is a workshop, filled with projects in progress lodged chummily together on two once-wide-open levels. (She added the second-floor "mezzanine" when she started making large, colorful rugs.) Cluttered around her and the welcome sunlight that shines through a windowed wall that reaches to the ceiling, are shelves and cabinets filled with the souvenirs, gifts, and flea market finds that stoke her poetic imagination—ragged toys, charming old games, storybooks, textile remnants, a cage of songbirds (to keep her company), and layer upon layer of the whimsical collections that have inspired her own bric-a-brac (also the name of one of her early books). Nathalie is a kind of one-woman Bauhaus working on five projects at the same time: a collection of ceramic mountains for an exhibit at Astier de Villatte; children's puzzles tucked in colorful re-creations of the Eiffel Tower (a recurring theme for her); whimsical children's books; paintings on glass and wood; knitted stuffed animals; rugs and pillows; tin boxes; textiles; printed T-shirts; painted bags; little jeweled hearts and flowers—many commissioned, yes, but always for herself as well.

This, then, is the world of Nathalie's work, her artistic playpen, only a minute's tree-lined walk from the world of her family life with Thomas, daughter Angéle, and son Oskar. That world, contained ("squished," she might say) in a similar amount of space as their double-decker studios, is a home that supports the domestic needs and shares the personal tastes

A bird's-eye view of Nathalie's playpen world. The tall windows give her constant sunlight, a view of her garden, and a place for the decorated cage of her songbirds and bric-a-brac.

of a strongly creative family. And though it is Nathalie through and through, it is not the home of Little Red Riding Hood.

When she was a little girl Nathalie's mother would dress her in a little red cape from her native Bavaria, a common sight there but not in Paris. With her big black dog walking beside her, people began to call her the Little Red Riding Hood of the neighborhood. If Nathalie were a writer, her nom de plume would be Little Red Riding Hood. If she drove an eighteen-wheeler, her trucker's handle might be Riding Hood, but since she is an artist, the romantic costume of her childhood has become a constant theme in her work. It has inspired the Little Red Riding Hood of her ceramics (see page 65), large, colorful Red Riding Hood rugs (see page 73), a book, and even a little animated Christmas movie she sent out as her holiday greeting one year. (You can see it on her Web site, www.Nathalie-lete.com or even on YouTube.)

Though she doesn't see her studio as a hideaway, it is and it isn't. It is in the sense that it's totally her place to do as she wishes, and to, as she puts it, "not be frustrated and to feel really free." It isn't in the sense that she can hear her husband's footsteps right above her working in his studio, and the children are always invited as well. In fact, to put a brake on her unstoppable passion to work,

"My studio space is where I can do what I want and feel really free"

—Nathalie

Opposite: In the middle of her colorful umbrella collection is a droopy sausage doll that played a part in Nathalie's fanciful kiosk exhibit on butchery.
Top: "Mama Doudou," an oversized fabric doll, hangs like the protective angel of the studio.
Bottom: A rainbow stack of Nathalie's hand-painted ceramic plates for Anthropologie.

A table alive with Nathalie's coral ceramics appears more like an imaginary seascape on the sandy floor of the ocean.

This page (clockwise from top right):
A giant knitted octopus guards the
entrance to the upstairs guest room; a
lineup of Nathalie's silk-screened and
hand-sewn cushions; from a pegboard
wall over Nathalie's desk dangles a
duo of funny fabric vegetables, along
with tools, prototypes, and inspiration (the chest of drawers on the left
was found on a street in Paris); three
hand-painted medallions float over
the guest-room bed.
Opposite: *A Little Red Riding Hood
rug and a bench of knitted bunnies,
bears, and pups welcome overnight
guests to a pastel heaven. The cozy
bed is layered with a patchwork cover
hand-sewn by the gifted hostess.*

she placed her daughter's piano in her studio. When Angéle finishes her evening practice, it is a signal for Nathalie to stop working and follow her daughter home.

A view from above of Nathalie's world today (see it on pages 66–67) explains her current predicament. When she first moved into the studio eight years ago it was "quite clear and empty, very beautiful and organized," she sighs. Her plan was to create artistic zones for all of her different kinds of work: the pottery near her kiln, the sewing and knitting projects on one table, the paintings and drawings on another. They would all be movable so she could rearrange the space as needed. Slowly the tables—her creative islands—got stuck with the physical weight of her mounting projects. Unlike some artists, she is not totally content working in her own creative clutter. Her dream is to begin again in a larger space with at least one Zen-like area with pristine white walls and an extra-long table. She thinks in a space like that, with no visual distraction or attachment to her past visual history, she might begin anew to create something she hasn't thought of yet. For an artist who has already explored so many forms of self-expression, what could that possibly be? "Wait and see," she laughs, as she dashes off to return to at least five projects that await her.

In what looks like a glass fish tank reside some of Nathalie's most cherished souvenirs and presents from around the world. The metal scrapbook wall behind it is covered with portraits and drawings by her children held fast by little magnets.

living with children

case history no. 3 **pamela bell**

How a mother of three transformed a beautifully dilapidated old town house by sharing all the decorating with her children.

pamela

Born in: Cincinnati, Ohio
Family: her children Elenore, 15,
Anabel, 13, Will, 10
Home: Lower East Side, New York City
Lived there: three years
Description: old brownstone built in 1748,
divided into several apartments
Challenge: to make a home that my children
would rather be in than anyplace else in the
world, and to focus on the important things
and not spend a fortune
Most hateful chore: taking the garbage out
House wish: I wanted this to be the house
my children and their friends always
wanted to come to
Just can't do it: go to sleep with a dirty
cup in the sink

Previous spread: A large-scale self-portrait of Will.
This page (clockwise from top): from left, Pamela, Elenore (standing), Anabel, and Will; the Art of the Sofa: To liven up a daughter's party and a plain muslin-covered sofa, Pamela passed around assorted fabric markers and paint pens to twelve-year-old would-be artists. The life of the party is seen opposite; the exterior of the house from the street.
Opposite: A view of the muslin-covered sofa that became a shared art project for friends and family. Above it twinkles the lights from a festive twig chandelier, originally hung as a temporary holiday decoration.

Pamela Bell never goes to bed leaving a dirty cup in the sink, "just the way I couldn't sleep in the shirt I've worn all day" she says. On the other hand, she prefers her sheets un-pressed and her silver un-polished. But to really understand Pamela Bell's home tactics, you only need to go as far as her big, airy living room to see the most honest expression of her housekeeping philosophy. Before two large twelve-foot windows facing out onto a quaint block of downtown New York City, sits a graceful sofa designed by none other than John Derian. Looking closer you squint your eyes trying to decide if the pattern on the white muslin cover is the same as the ubiquitous scribbles most often observed in subway tunnels and on construction site fences—graffiti! Pamela explains that a year had gone by and she still couldn't decide what to upholster the sofa with, so one evening when her daughter Elenore (older sister of Anabel and Will) had a party and some of her friends were sitting in a corner looking kind of left out, Mom spontaneously grabbed a handful of fabric pens and stirred up the crowd with, "Do you guys want to paint the couch?" In a minute the pens were gone and the sofa became the life of the party! Ever since then, whenever young and not-so-young friends stop by the pens are passed out to add a peace sign or another stylized signature to the sofa's crazy maze of colorful hieroglyphics. It's become the family's super-sized guest book. This pretty much sums up the way Pamela feels about sharing her home with her children. "It's ours, not mine," she declares. (Their father, Alex, lives around the corner.) When Will asked if he could paint a pair of the living room's armchairs, muslin cousins to the reborn sofa, Mom welcomed his creative initiative and handed over the fabric paint and brushes. The back cushion of one now bears his freestyle version of a Star Wars coat of arms. This laissez-faire approach to letting the children have such a personal hand in the look of their home has supported their pride of ownership. They each chose the paint color of their rooms and the fabric for the curtains. Anabel and a friend went a step further and painted her room themselves.

Pamela has always wished for "this to be the house my children and their friends always wanted to come to." So far, so good. She attributes its popularity to an overall welcoming spirit provided first by her children—"they're great hosts"—as well as a supply of good snacks and, for the past couple of years, her presence. Most of the other mothers go to work, and until a couple of years ago when her business with Kate Spade and two other partners was sold, she did too. Now she's working on her own fashion and design projects, plus a pilot cooking school, sharing with the children a cozy white-brick-walled work and study space on the ground floor. Dominating the room are two slightly contradictory objects: a graphic red and white poster issued by the British government at the start of World War II—"Keep Calm and Carry On"—and a huge tabletop calendar with every day filled in—a less than calm schedule of activities. What both reflect is a high-gear

Opposite: When passersby on the street look through Pamela's floor-to-ceiling window, they see a sparkly disco ball and a dancing bear. The sequined ball once decorated a holiday store window; the painting of the bear, affectionately known as Simon, along with the Mexican tablecloth's yellow sunflowers, bring a little bit of country inside.
Left: A colorful toy top from Istanbul.

This page (clockwise from top left): The children's art is given prominence on a set of little shelves in the playroom; hand-painted upholstery by Will; a family scrapbook on view; a bold neon welcome to Will's bedroom.
Opposite: *Ten-year-old Will's hand-painted "Stars Wars" chair sits proudly on view in the main living room.*

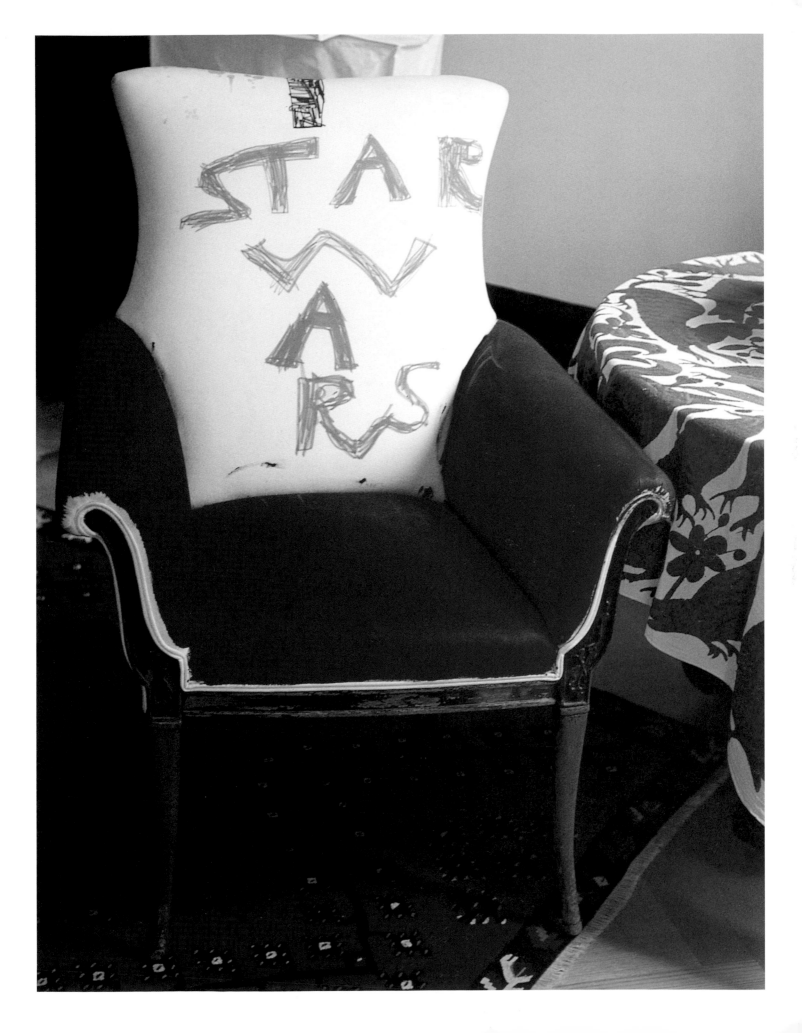

energy re-ignited daily by a home that in-spires not only self-expression and creativity, but warmth and security surrounded by the familiar mementos of a life built together like a big, colorful scrapbook.

Three years ago, on a midnight hunt surfing the internet for real estate, Pamela and her children received a chance for a different kind of do-it-together lifestyle. She spied an ad for a slightly dilapidated, timeworn four-story brick beauty built in the mid-eighteenth century, within walking distance of the children's school. When she first walked in she saw past the mess. "The halls were covered with some kind of blue bumpy stucco," she recalled. "But when I looked up the staircase and held on to the old banister and felt the width of the house, I thought I was going to die from hap-piness. My friends thought I was crazy, but for me it was instantaneous. I could see it all."

The house had been carved into several apartments, but she did only what she had to do, adding one bathroom and leaving the stuff that requires a lot of time. The children saw it right after she bought it, and not again until the night they moved in. "It was right before Christmas and some friends helped me string lights all through the house," she reminisces, "so that when we arrived after dark, it was all lit up." She had made sure all their favorite things were moved in so they felt at home from the start. A leftover from that night, a bunch of branches entwined with strings of lights, still dangles from the ceiling. One day she'll buy a real chandelier, but for now it lights their way just fine.

Opposite: On Elenore's wall, works by Wendy Small, Pam Butler, and Justine Kurland (gifts from Mom) mingle with her own artistic endeavors.
Top: A faux cardboard chandelier hangs over her bed.
Bottom: In Anabel's bedroom, in front of a work by Nina Bovasso, sprouts a very organized still life.

The paraphernalia of a young beauty,
thirteen-year-old Anabel, laid out neatly on a
low vintage table. Bottles and tubes of health
and beauty aids mixed with charger cords,
journals, collected boxes, tickets, a shiny green
alligator, and a miniature bouquet of roses
from the garden bring to mind a perfect still
life for a modern-day Matisse.

Clockwise from top left: Pamela's favorite place to write—a little country chair and table facing a wall of purple-flocked wallpaper and a view of the neighborhood; in a wallpapered nook right outside Pamela's bedroom, a prim little French boudoir chair once covered in pale blue damask now lives more dangerously covered in an antique marriage cloth bought at an Istanbul market; a bedside table-to-go made of a stack of vintage suitcases; displayed on Pamela's bedroom desk, seen above, a Batman Pez dispenser and a ceramic quasi Batmobile created by Will. Priceless!
Opposite: While others choose to hide their TVs, Pamela exhibits hers right out in the open surrounded by an eclectic collection of art and photography.

motherly tips

Priceless Gifts for Children: You don't have to wait until your children have grown up to give them grown-up gifts. On every other birthday, Pamela picks out something special to give her three children. For Elenore's fifteenth birthday it was a painting, a large, handwritten love letter by Michael Skokins (seen on page 100). It hangs in the upstairs TV room right now, but when she moves into her own place someday she will have a little collection to call her own (as will Anabel and Will).

I wish I had been as smart as Pamela, but maybe I'm getting better. Lately I've been giving the newborns in our family vintage editions of my favorite classics—*The Secret Garden*, *Charlotte's Web*, *The Wind in the Willows*—well, you get the picture. Two Christmases ago my mother personally inscribed an anthology of Robert Louis Stevenson poems to give each of her eighteen grandchildren. Above each inscription she tacked in a beautiful old sepia photograph of her mother, who died when she was a little girl and was distantly related to the author. One day, hopefully, the grandchildren's children will pull it from a shelf of their home library and say, "Daddy, Mommy, who is this beautiful lady who has the same last name of the author of *Treasure Island*?" Now that's what I call priceless.

Romancing the Home: In several places in Pamela's house you will find a comely stack of vintage suitcases. "I just love the design—their squareness," she says. The trio piled up next to her bed serves as a bedside table. The quartet in the living room is an altar of sorts to sacred books. "I love the idea of travel when you actually had to carry a suitcase. It's just romantic to me. There's something about the whole experience of travel, especially train travel. I love the scene in *Out of Africa* when Isak Dinesen gets off the train with her stack of gorgeous suitcases." Though Pamela keeps nothing inside of hers, there's plenty of room to store children's artwork, old letters, school papers, and saved magazines and newspaper articles . . . on travel, perhaps!

It was Pamela's son who came up with the idea of storing their sleeping bags inside the gold-colored leather poufs (Moroccan-style bean bag chairs, seen on page 216) they had brought back from a souk in Morocco. They sit in a cluster in the Bells' living room ready to provide extra seating at a moment's notice, and they're portable as well.

Freedom of Choice: Giving your children some role in decorating their home or at least their own space, even if it's just choosing the bedspreads on their beds, gives them a sense of pride and ownership. When it comes to painting their rooms, take them with you to the paint store and let them choose some paint chips. If you are trying to work within a certain color theme, limit their choices within a range of colors, say blues, but let them choose which blue they like.

Child Proud: Display your children's school projects out in the open, not just in their bedrooms. Pamela integrates her children's artwork with that of well-known artists. It sits on her desk, in her bedroom, on a special scrapbook board in the family room. It not only makes children proud, but it sends a strong message about your support for their school and their teachers. "I do anything I

Right: Family comings and goings are captured, shared, and constantly updated with brightly colored markers in a mega-sized monthly calendar.
Opposite: In the creative mayhem of the ground-floor workroom/study shared by Pamela and her children is a framed message from Great Britain's Ministry of Information (1939). It has become an on-again off-again family motto.

can to show them how important their education is to me."

Scrapbook Walls: Pamela has always loved this great way to save your walls and give your children a special place to hang their artwork and personal memorabilia. Go to your local art supply store and pick up a large sheet of foam core, cover it with a happy fabric, and push pin photos, children's artwork, postcards, cutouts, and more.

Living without Boundaries: It is Pamela's belief that if children are given the freedom and the tools to explore their creativity within the home, they will self-regulate and never be destructive. "I gave my children permission to draw on our sofa. Will asked me if he could decorate the chairs in the living room. If there is something they want to do they ask. Usually the answer is yes." If they feel it's their home, why would they want to damage it?

Time Out: "I used to go to work and come home. Now my work and my life with my children are one. Sometimes I need time to myself so in that big calendar I oversee for all of us, I am slowly building in time for me! I am thinking of planning two weeks a year where I can take off and do something for myself."

> "I wanted this to be the house my children and their friends always wanted to come to"
>
> —Pamela

Opposite: Children's artwork—a superhero shield and papier-mâché mask—prominently displayed on a contemporary glass table.
Top: A hand-crafted message from Will to his mom on her bedroom bulletin board.
Bottom: Will and his pals often hang out in his bright orange (his choice!) room, featuring handy pegboard storage and a loft for creating Lego structures and other "do not disturb" projects.

Comfort

Curled up in cushioned chairs,
pillowed chaises, and soft sofas
with a favorite book, a pet, and a
soft blanket for warmth.

For me, a comfortable house is one that feels like a favorite pair of slippers worn in to fit your foot perfectly, like a pair of woolly socks. Comfort is born out of use, therefore the most comfortable houses seem to be the ones that have been most lived in. In a fashion review in the *New York Times* in March 2009, Cathy Horyn wrote that the architect Rem Koolhaas was asked how creativity may be influenced by the recession. He said one result could be more projects that focus on the social rather than on the private sector. Koolhaas also noted that in New York he has sensed a shift from "civilization to comfort." "Rather than smart," he said, "things have to be more comfortable.'"

When I curl up in the corner of my favorite sofa with a soft fleece blanket wrapped around me, sipping a cup of hot tea and with piles of books and magazines strewn around and a concerto playing softly in the background, I can't help but think of some of Jane Austen's characters, like Lady Bertram in *Mansfield Park*, who retreated to dainty chaises and wrapped themselves up in soft coverlets with a small pug or two at hand. The other novelist who comes to mind is Laurie Colwin. She, like Austen, seemed to relish the art of comfort and gave us wonderful examples of how to serve it up. In *Happy All the Time*, her heroine, Holly Sturgis, is pegged by her head-over-heels-lover, Guido Morris, as "a strong domestic sensualist" and someone who knew a thing or two about creating comfort. "She had a positive genius for comfort but he was only a visitor: that comfort

had been created long before he met her."

Comfort has nothing to do with the decorating style of a house, nor its age. Take a look at the cozy, cluttered style of Natalie Gibson's ancient row house in London (Case History No. 7, page 189) and contrast it with the more minimal style of Pamela Bell's in New York City (Case History No. 3, page 77). Both are comfortable in their own way. Natalie's sofa in her front parlor (her favorite place to lie when no one's around) is an altar to comfort layered with fuzzy kitten pillows, patchwork quilts, and colorful Indian textiles. The big white overstuffed sofa tumbled with pillows and usually a child or two in the TV room at the Bells' residence is just as comfortable. The place of comfort for Elena Salgueiro (Case History No. 4, page 105) is the chair next to her bed. It is draped in a Venetian tablecloth—dragonflies and flowers from a stray fabric sample. The really comforting thing is the light that warms the chair from the large casement windows nearby that are according to Elena, "always open and always slamming," and the pile of books it supports, some transient and some permanent, like the old weathered copy of *Kristin Lavransdatter*, an unfinished garden diary, and two books on plant recipes by Francois Couplan. Oberto Gili (Case History No. 1, page 31) is most comfortable sitting in a chair at his kitchen table or one of his desks. He never sits in an armchair or on a sofa, even to read a book. My sister Liza's comfort zone (Case History No. 6, page 161) is in her kitchen standing in front of her marble work counter with flour up to her elbows or stirring an untried sauce

at her stove. The next best thing would be sitting at the writing table in her upstairs study researching new recipes from the hundreds of cookbooks piled up around her and stored in the shelves nearby. It's no surprise that Geri Roper (Case History No. 5, page 133) is most comfortable in bed surrounded by her dogs. The most comfortable room in her house is home to their four crates, their canvas-covered doggy beds, baskets of their stuffed animals and show ribbons, a big wooden dining table, a fireplace, and the kitchen. It's the room everyone—four-legged and two-legged—gravitates to.

A comfort rebellion took place in our house in the country a couple of years ago. My husband and two sons were tired of my collection of wobbly, uncomfortable furniture—chairs, benches, stools—but most of all the lack of a comfortable sofa to stretch out on. Our old porch swing seemed to address their needs during the summer, but when the weather cooled and life moved inside they were forced to read their books and newspapers upright. I had no chance—three against one (even our dog Charley sided with them)—so in the end a sofa (a new one) was found and replaced a wonderful old sideboard in front of the fire.

When did this need for comfortable furniture arise? The ancient Egyptians seemed fine resting their heads on wooden blocks instead of pillows. In the Middle Ages, even chairs (hard ones) were a rare commodity. If there was one it was the lord of the manor who sat in it, and that's where our first "chairman" came from. (No mention of

Previous spread: Dogs have a nose for comfort.
Opposite: There is nothing like the comfort of a soft blanket.
Left: Priceless comforts: favorite socks, a squishy bedroom chaise, and reading the Sunday newspaper!

Who wouldn't want to dive into this over-stuffed sofa complete with a supply of reading material? Actually there's one, its owner Oberto Gili, who is more comfortable sitting at his kitchen table. To each his own kind of comfort!

> ## "Comfort is born out of use, therefore the most comfortable houses seem to be the ones that have been lived in."

a "chairwoman" of course!) The first feather mattress didn't show up until the sixteenth century. Up until then you were lucky to sleep on one made of straw. The first upholstered (padded and covered) chairs trickled in during the seventeenth century, and only to comfort the already padded seats of the wealthy. And it wasn't until 1680 that the first real armchair appeared. In Victorian times, furniture began to be mass-produced; everyman and everywoman could now sink into a comfy couch or sofa, just like my three men and a dog.

A comfortable home reveals the personal side of our day-to-day living. It is an intimate view that is not always perfect—a few dishes in the sink, the dog on the sofa, a child's coloring project left on the dining room table, books piled up, slippers kicked off, a mantelpiece cluttered with bric a brac.

The Swedish artist Carl Larsson made the everyday life of his wife Karin and their seven children the subject of his most famous watercolors (see one on page 19, top right). Instead of idealizing everything in its place, he painted what he saw: the dog asleep on the parlor floor, cast-off slippers, a rumpled sofa scattered with newspapers. These are the frames of a home movie shot by a doting father and an artist who focused his lens on the comforts of the real and unadorned home.

Opposite: This is comfort—a T-shirt you can hide in, bare feet on the furniture, and a TV remote control all to yourself!
Left: The elements of comfort include an old chaise lounge covered in a soft cotton blanket backed up with a collection of "sunny" hand-embroidered throw pillows.

A Nose For Comfort

Dogs have a nose for comfort. Ours always sniffed out the most comfortable spots in our homes. In the city there were three: the sofa, and an old wing chair in the living room, and a chaise lounge in our bedroom. In the country, it was another wing chair in the kitchen, and two armchairs in the living room, and most recently, the new sofa in the dining room. There's also our beds. It always seemed like the dogs got there first, and since they asked for so little we rarely had the heart to displace them. There were times, though, out of desperation—to watch a football game or movie in comfort—we might lure them down with a treat and then race back to claim their spot. All's fair in love and the pursuit of comfort!

If you let sleeping pets lie—on your furniture or on comfy rugs and carpeting—you'll wish for the gift one of my dog-loving pals once sent us: a big box filled with every size of lint roller for picking up that ubiquitous dog hair. Another friend recommended Zero Odor, a non-toxic biodegradable spray that eliminates odors without leaving a scent behind. The idea is to spray it on your dog's bed, not on the dog.

Most pets really love having their own home—crate or bed. Obviously, they won't park themselves there 24/7, they get bored just like us. But a good comfy dog bed with a zip-off cover is an excellent alternative to your chaise longue, and it's washable! Vacuum the carpets your pets lounge on as often as possible. Sprinkle a little baking soda on the area first! It's a great odor absorber.

Charley, our black Lab, always got first dibs at the most comfortable spots in the house, including our living room sofa camouflaged with folk art pillows and an eclectic mix of antique coverlets.

103

living with memory

case history no. 4 **elena salgueiro**

How a woman with a dream to live in an old house transformed a new one (inside and out) through a patina of heirlooms, family photographs, paint, and plants, thanks to an obstinate passion.

elena

Born in: Moscow
Family: her husband Daniel, and their children Ksenia, 12, Alice, 8, Tom, 6, Nella, 4, Diane, 1 month
Home: Thomery, France
Lived there: six years
Description: one of the most plain buildings erected in the fifties in very agreeable surroundings, but totally lacking what old houses come by naturally—character, patina, and generations of living
Challenge: to deal with a house neither really old (fifty-nine, a house in menopause), nor really new, but just so perfectly plain
Solutions: dreams, people, and junk, which is a way of saving memories and feeling they are all at your side, your familiar spirits
Inspiration: my own experience, tastes, and the strong desire to keep memories of everything I do not want to lose. And my dreams that keep me afloat.

Previous spread: A tale called "My Friends," written and illustrated by an eight-year-old Elena, which rests on a photo of her best supporters, her parents, on their wedding day.
Clockwise from top: Elena in the shadow of the wisteria tunnel that leads up to the main entrance of her home, seen opposite; on Elena's wrists a pair of broken watches, "an altar to her dear folks, now out of time" (the smaller one belonged to her great-aunt Katerina and the big one to her grandfather); a living memory—a sketch from the boyhood diary of Elena's father.

Over time, really old houses take on patinas that sustain and support their character. Brand-new houses have something else—not patina, exactly, but a purity of design that becomes a backdrop for the individuality of those who dwell within. But how to deal with a house that is neither old nor really new? That was the challenge for Elena Salgueiro when she and her husband Daniel and their then two young children (they now have five) moved from an apartment in Paris to a plain little house near the historic village of Fontainebleau. Built in the fifties, it had nothing to commend it, except some beautiful old trees and ancient stone walls defining its rather snug borders. Even the ground around it had been suffocated with gravel laid by the former owner, who wanted nothing to do with the possibility of overgrown grass or worse, weeds! She was, according to Elena, "a brave old lady, a real housekeeper, not at all a homemaker. Though everything was in the most perfect order, it oozed the most perfect boredom."

In defiance, Elena and Daniel, and even their children scraped, composted and planted whatever growing things Elena fell in love with—even evil nettles! They put the bathroom where the kitchen had been and the kitchen in the garage, and then connected them with a brand-new circular staircase that now looks as if at least three generations have trod up and down it. That was Elena's dream from the start, and now her "ugly duckling" house, as she once described it,

Opposite: The upstairs entrance guarded with signs of footless life, a Christmas wreath, and a tangle of jackets and hats overseen by a cozy mix of family photos and paintings.
Top: Welcoming touches—an old straw hat and a basket of herbs—at the ground-floor entrance.
Bottom: In the backyard, Ksenia's little hand-built lean-to provides a natural hideaway for her creativity.

has that missing patina. It was created from the borrowed memories of the secondhand treasures she collected from a handful of favorite neighborhood "half antique/half rummage" shops. These include: the slightly worn chairs and tables camouflaged with thoughtfully placed shawls and coverlets; the piles and shelves of storybooks, art books, and novels in French, English, and Russian; the rescued pair of portraits hanging side by side in the living room over a pair of mismatched clocks christened "Cinderella" and "Theodor" that have never ticked off a second; the photographs of real family members romantically preserved in sepia and carved wooden frames and albums—and as abundant as the plants thriving in nooks and crannies everywhere—exude an ever-evolving, far-from-make-believe heritage. The background music to these artful tableaux, a little like scenes from an Agnès Varda movie, is supplied by the deft fingers of the children on the keys of the family's prized piano—they were taught by their mother and use old yellowed scores of Bach and Tchaikovsky, among others—and a constant hum generated by the creative energy of this family's unique kind of living. They had no big budget; everything was done, says Elena "at the expense of spirit, allowing our taste to adapt to the possibilities of the place."

A glance at Elena's hand-drawn map of the family's eight-hundred-square-meter kingdom, reaffirms how two adults and five children have accomplished so much living

Above: In the upstairs hallway family photos are displayed on a barrel-like wooden piece called a "maie" (supposedly its original use was for storing crockery). Next to it is a collection of old canes and umbrellas.
Opposite: According to Elena, "the English library loyally supports a bottomless amphora, an empty golden cage, piles of books, invasive plants, and all the cracks on the ceiling," which she loves.

Opposite: The stairway down to the kitchen level is not the old one Elena dreamed of but one made from a new natural birch that is generously waxed and now well trod.

Clockwise from top left: A desk meant for "Papa" is often taken over with children's projects; the kitchen table is always set like a Rembrandt still life with "things that need to be at hand and cannot be put anywhere else," which is how Elena puts it— fresh vegetables and fruits, breads from the oven, and dishes ready for the table; a little bookcase in the parlor attached to the kitchen once was a place to store food; Tom takes a nap on a comforting little "couchette" with a view of the garden.

In a corner of the library, little Nella, watched over by a vintage toy monkey, entertains her-self with favorite family storybooks on a sofa padded with patchwork quilts and a collection of assorted pillows.

in such a compact space. And though a lot of it is shared, no one seems deprived of a place to call his or her own—either inside or out. It's a good thing too, because each of the children seems to have inherited (mostly from their mother) an acquisitive nature. Even twelve-year-old Ksenia, the oldest, has created a backyard hut (seen on page 109) to escape to for reading, drawing, dreaming, and enjoying her stuff.

So, did anyone ever caution the heroine of this real-life story, our Case History No.

"…beautiful homes bring up beautiful people, in every sense of the word."

—Elena

4, to be careful what you wish for? She dreamed up her home, filled it with the abandoned goods of other people's lives, rejected the perfect housekeeping standards of the woman who lived in it for fifty-four years before her, opted for imagination over monotony, overruled perfection for authenticity, and out of necessity accepted her role as "housekeeper," but in spirit is a "homemaker." Home for her is inspired by experience, tastes, and the strong desire to keep memories of everything she does not want to lose. She believes fervently in intimacy and comfort and asserts with her philosophical Russian soul, "that beautiful homes bring up beautiful people, in every sense of the word."

Opposite: After the garage was turned into a kitchen, the former dining room became the library and the dining table a perfect place for reading, drawing, and playing games.
Top: Alice in the library/living room making moves on a treasured chess set inscribed to her grandfather on his birthday in 1965.
Bottom: Elena and Alice play a duet.

117

It's hard to believe this romantic ground-floor parlor, a place for the family to take time out for a little old-fashioned creativity, demonstrated by Tom and Alice, was once a concrete garage. Its transformation started in Elena's head on her very first visit.

Welcomes

A light in the window, a wreath on the door, a mat that reads Welcome— making friends and family feel at home even before the warm hugs inside the doorway, be it twelve stories up or through a garden gate.

he old red bike parked outside Oberto Gili's front door is his hello and goodbye to friends who arrive and depart from the ground-floor entrance of the West Village brownstone he has lived in for fifteen years. The large sequined styrofoam globe that can be seen floating in the air through the second-story window over the front door of Pamela Bell's old brick townhouse was hung the first Christmas she and her three children moved in. Now it welcomes friends and family, and attracts the attention of any passerby who spies it (there are no curtains on the windows) all year-round. What used to be the garage to the fifty-four-year-old house in Thomery, France, inhabited by the six Salgueiros—Elena and Daniel, four daughters, and a son—was fearlessly transformed into a cozy kitchen, a family room, a bedroom for two of the girls, and a laundry room. Its entrance, a sliding glass door crowned by dangling wisteria vines trailing down from the balcony above, is reached by a gravel footpath edged with all manner of blooming things—nettles, ferns, and wildflowers— some of them sprouting from odd crockery pots, a pewter goblet, old straw baskets, and whatever treasured junk pieces Elena and the children have added that day. Though it's not the real entrance to the house (that's around the corner and up a stairway), it seems the most welcoming one, as evidenced by the posse of cast-off muddied sandals and shoes ringing the tile-paved terrace before it. On the bright blue Moroccan door of one of

the oldest entranceways in London, circa 1650, a not-so-old brass letterbox bears a fairly new, not very welcoming handwritten message: "Please! No Junk Mail, Pizza Giveaway or Cab Cards." Natalie Gibson, who has resided there since 1963, attributes the aforementioned threat to her husband Jon Wealleans, who grew tired of unwelcome junk mail slid through their handy mail slot. His gruff request belies his gentlemanly demeanor, but even English hospitality has its limits. These three tales of welcome and one of woe, extracted from the case histories documented throughout this book, recommend how personal spontaneity—an old red bike, a sequined disco ball—can become the most tantalizing icebreakers in making a house a home, not only for those of us who hold our doors wide open, but for those who pass through.

A Country Welcome

On nights when we are expecting our grown-up children or weekend guests to arrive at Elm Glen Farm, our old farmhouse in upstate New York, I practice my lifetime ritual of lighting candles to welcome them. I dim the electric candlelights of the kitchen chandelier, and beneath it on a long country table light a chorus line of votive candles each in their own little ironstone dish. Outside I light more candles protected from the wind by a collection of old and new lanterns. Two hang in the old lilac tree that guards the door to the kitchen, which was not intended to be the official entrance but has been for the twenty years we have lived here. The tree

blesses us in early summer with its intoxicating old-fashioned scent. The other lanterns rest nearby on the cracked surface of a green-and-white-tile bistro table that barely survives the inappropriate snow that covers it winter after winter. The headlights from the arriving cars are a signal to my husband Howard that it's time to head outside with a flashlight (or hop into our vintage golf cart) for a personal greeting and the stowing of luggage, as I wait in the doorway yelling encouraging "Hello"s from behind him.

> "Nothing beats a personal greeting,
> a warm hug or an excited
> barking dog, for getting a dinner
> or party off to a great start."

A City Welcome

If you live your life in an apartment, you can't light lanterns along a stone path to welcome your guests from the elevator to your front door (not that I haven't thought about it!), but there are ways to personalize an urban hallway.

On the Door:

When Natalie Gibson and Jon Wealleans came to visit a few months ago, I taped a picture of them on our door—they were standing in their front door in Bermondsy (see it on page 190)—with a big "Welcome Natalie and Jon" scribbled under it. Before they rang the bell, I heard their laughter! This Thanksgiving we welcomed thirty-five people (nineteen of whom were family) to a sit-down turkey dinner. Since you can't

Previous spread: The best welcome of all is a warm hug at the door.
Opposite: A posse of cast-off muddied sandals and shoes outside a well-trodden entrance.
Left: Some apartment buildings allow their tenants to create a homey feeling outside their doors with the welcoming touch of a painting, a mirror, or a decorative side table. But nothing beats a happy, panting dog.

hammer a nail into an apartment front door, hanging a bittersweet or cranberry wreath is a bit of a challenge. I tried one of those handy metal wreath hangers that hook over the top of the door, but unfortunately it created a larger challenge— closing it! Instead, I rigged it with a piece of coarse string pulling it over the top of the door and securing it to the door knob inside. Another charming door warmer is a child's drawing. Having two young great-nephews and a niece as Thanksgiving artists-in-residence, our entire door became a makeshift gallery for their pilgrim- and turkey-themed art.

At the Door:

A doormat serves an obvious purpose at the entrance of a house. We pause and press off a little dew from a morning walk; we scrape thick mud from a soggy tramp up and down the mountain; we knock off crunchy snow after carrying an armload of logs from the woodshed. In the city there's little left to press or scrape or wipe clean after we've traveled through the lobby and up the elevator, and yet there is something so welcoming about a doormat outside an apartment door. It's a reminder that an apartment is a home, too. And whether it has Welcome inscribed on it or not, the message is inherent.

The door to our twelfth-floor apartment is situated in a little cul-de-sac right off of the elevator. With just one other (very friendly!) neighbor right next door, on special occasions we have the opportunity to take advantage of this atypical geography and relationship to extend the borders of our entranceway beyond our front door. Some-

times we place an antique chair near the door or a little table displaying a funny toy. To celebrate a book by Oberto Gili, we leaned against the wall outside a framed blowup of a ripply image he had taken of an American flag painted in the bottom of his swimming pool in Italy.

The Best Welcome of All

The best welcomes are waiting just inside the door. Nothing beats a warm hug and a personal greeting from a friend, a child, or an excited barking dog for getting a visit, a dinner, or a party off to a good start. Don't worry about the last-minute preparations or making sure everything is absolutely in its place. You can light the candles, put the hors d'oeuvres out, pick up whatever it is you're worrying about after you've warmly welcomed your guests. Or even better, let them help. It's the best way to make your friends feel at home, not like guests.

Oberto Gili's old red two-wheeler propped in front of his wood supply outside the front door of his brownstone in New York City. The bike is a welcome sign that its owner is home.

Welcome Home

"You Can't Go Home Again," Thomas Wolfe told us. But for those of us who are fortunate enough to have some vestige of our childhood home to go to, we can and we do. It may not be exactly the way we remembered it, but our imaginations fill in the elements that are missing—the spirit and the people. The first welcome to Muskettoe Pointe Farm, my home for almost three decades, is the tree-lined sandy lane that greets you as you turn the car through the two carved fence posts. The old weathered fence leads the way under a leafy canopy of old cedars, bayberries, and hollies. I hear the hoofbeats of our ragtag herd of black-faced sheep, our brown pony Blue Tail, her sidekick Scrabble, and Soul Sister, the burro. The sun has set and as the house comes into view I see through the dining room windows the candlelight shining from the tin chandeliers nailed to the old wooden beams in the ceiling. I hear the faint sound of music from the stereo hidden in the Queen Anne cabinet next to the upright piano, and an off-key chorus singing, "We are family . . . I've got all my sisters and me . . ." The kitchen door opens and I see the silhouettes of my mother and father and a crowd of dancing children behind them, and now I can hear the happy barking of Saint and Zena, our boisterous Saint Bernards. "Welcome, home! Welcome, home!"

A sandy tree-lined lane provides a first warm embrace as you make your way to the house and the greetings that await you.

9/26/93

It's appel time ♥

FALL

uy Randolph. M.

A Welcome Book

Memories don't take up space! Elena Salgueiro would disagree, since she has saved memories and created a history for her relatively new house through the discarded treasures of others—books, chairs, paintings, china, and the childhood diaries of her father. But, let me restate my "saving memories" case! How can we physically save the memory of times shared with people we love, who we invite into our home for a visit, a meal, a tea, a weekend? One simple way is to create a personal welcome book, a place for your friends to share a memory of their visit in your home. Pick up one of those simple books with the blank pages, divide it into the seasons, and on a special occasion pass it around to your friends. I have kept them for years, filled not only with the names of guests and special inscriptions, but photographs, children's drawings, and even the menus of special dinners. My books are bulging now, but that's okay. Friends enjoy being part of your history, especially grownup children, nieces, and nephews who love to look back and see their childish handwriting and their drawings, which were so naive but often so perceptive.

A page from our welcome book at Elm Glen Farm, which stores personal greetings, pictures, and memories. The day we planted our "appel" tree, my then-young niece Mary Randolph Norton recorded the event.

living with dogs

case history no. 5 geri roper

Meet the woman who shares her comfortable house (and sometimes her bed!) with four rambunctious spaniels, as well as their crates, cushions, toys, dog hair, and love.

geri

Born in: Houston, Texas
Family: her husband Jim, their children
Whitney, James, Jeb, and Willy, and the dogs,
Henry, Elle, Wylie, and Dash
Home: Rumson, New Jersey
Lived there: twenty-six years
Description: an old barn built in
the twenties
Challenges: making it a home everybody
loves—children, dogs, and friends.
Getting rid of stuff.
Solution: keeping the stuff that matters
—photographs of the children and lots of
books everywhere
Best feature: its informality
Worst: her clutter
Words to live by: dogs never lie
about love
A perfect house? To her, absolutely
because it's alive

Previous spread: Making themselves at home, even on the light-colored carpeting of the front hall, are the Ropers' spaniels—Henry (the clumber), Wylie, Elle, and Dash (all springers).

This page (clockwise from top): Geri as a young mom with Whitney; "keep off the furniture" doesn't apply in this house, where chairs and cushions are covered in washable canvas covers; a picture of a clumber spaniel like Henry keeps watch over Geri's proud mother doggy necklace.

Opposite: Signs of dog life: a well-chewed teddy bear dropped on the hall floor along with a partially chewed (compliments of Henry) gilt-framed portrait of a clumber.

To start with there are Whitney, James, Jeb, and Willy. Then there are Henry, Elle, Wylie, and Dash. They're all Geri Roper's children—except the last four are her doggy children, her three springer spaniels (Elle, Wylie, and Dash) and Henry, her clumber spaniel. They all live together in what started out as an old barn, circa 1920, that Geri and her husband Jim discovered in Rumson, New Jersey, soon after they were married.

Over the years, twenty-six now, they've added on to it many times. "At first we didn't get it right," explains Geri. "It was more a house for adults. But as we became a family (four children in five years!) the house became a family house. We all grew up in it together." "All" includes the dogs (as many as six at one time), several horses, and at least one cat. According to Geri, they all get along fine. "I've never had a lot of rules for my kids or my dogs. And, so far, they've all turned out really well."

Since the children are now grown and away most of the time—two in college, one in medical school, and one working in New York City—the house has transitioned into more of a, well, dogs' house. In the large sunny kitchen cum family room, there's plenty of evidence that dogs rule. Mixed in with the light-colored comfy canvas sofas and chairs are big squishy dog beds, dog

"I think I am a better at making a house warm, than keeping it organized."

—Geri

Opposite: The simplicity of the dogs' crates keeps them unobtrusive against the light-colored floors and canvas-covered furniture of the Ropers' airy living room.
Top: Dash snoozes on one of the comfy canvas pillows strewn throughout the house.
Bottom: Henry loves his crate. On top is a basket filled with dog-show ribbons.

137

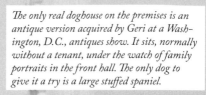

The only real doghouse on the premises is an antique version acquired by Geri at a Washington, D.C., antiques show. It sits, normally without a tenant, under the watch of family portraits in the front hall. The only dog to give it a try is a large stuffed spaniel.

crates, dog toys, dog teddies, dog books, pictures of dogs, baskets of dog-show ribbons, and a little throw pillow with a message in needlepoint, Dogs never lie about love, which Geri swears sounds so trite, but is so true.

Just inside the front door is an early folk art doghouse (reportedly the dogs have never been in it) and in the dining room hangs a handsome Vermont hooked rug bearing likenesses of former Roper spaniels, Lennie, Higgins, Liza, and Lily. The only room in the house that's off-limits to the furry family members is, ironically, the most unlived-in room in the house—the living room. "We only seem to use it at Christmas," Geri admits, "so it doesn't really matter to them." When she heads in that direction, they all plop down on the carpet a few yards away patiently awaiting her return. When day is done, they follow her upstairs. On the nights when Jim is in the city, all four pile onto their bed. "Actually, they pile in first and I have to find a place among them," she says.

It would seem that a house filled with dogs and children and all the things that go along with each would not have much room for other things. But not in Geri's world. "I love being surrounded by things that have significance to me," she says. Besides the kids and dogs, she's got an unquenchable thirst for oversized illustrated books; all kinds of photographs, many tracing the seasons of her children, and many of horses (her daughter has ridden since childhood); and all kinds

of unusual handmade frames. She loves to match frames to pictures, but sometimes doesn't get around to hanging them. They lean on walls, and are propped against, and stacked on or under, benches waiting for a home. The wait could be long, but that seems to be the laissez-faire code of this home— everything in its own time and first things first—like making sure everyone's comfortable, fed, and happy. Another thing she's not gotten around to is hanging curtains. Though she likes the way they can finish a room and provide privacy, she much prefers unfettered views and lots of light flooding in even on the gloomiest day. "We don't need any privacy here because where we live there's no one looking in our windows, except possibly an occasional deer!"

"I think I'm better at making a house warm than keeping it organized," Geri confesses. "I think people feel welcome here because it's informal and lived-in. Sometimes I have my girlfriends come over in their nightgowns or pajamas." She admits that not everyone embraces her clutter and the four big dogs running around. "There are people that like everything very orderly and in its place all the time. When people like that come here they make me a little nervous and vice versa. There are others who think it's cool, but they would never live like this themselves." This is a house that once was a barn and now is a home because of all the people and pets that have lived in it just the way they wanted to. "I think it's a good home because it's alive," Geri says. "There's always activity and dogs, dogs, and dogs!"

Right: Wylie and Elle's dog-show spoils are stored in a wicker basket.
Opposite: Bedtime stories for the four-legged children of this family topped by a portrait of a springer named Jackson.

When it's bedtime, Dash, Henry, Wylie, and Elle head upstairs and pile into bed, usually ahead of the family member who will be challenged to find a spot!

it's ok to sleep with your dog

I have watched my six-foot-three-inch son get down on the floor and nestle beside our fourteen-year-old black Lab Charley resting on her large pillow bed. Charley used to be able to bound up on his bed, but arthritis and all those problems that limit activities of old dogs, and old people as well, have put a stop to that. Some nights when she is sleeping on the floor next to my side of the bed, I watch her. Every once in a while when she twitches and makes those little sleeping-dog noises, I wonder if she's dreaming about jumping up in my son's bed or up on the front seat of his blue pick-up, where she used to love to ride with her head on his lap or leaning out the back window. I think so.

Before Charley we had Bo, a wild and wiley wire-haired fox terrier. Though he loved to sleep in our bed, particularly when the afternoon sun hit it, he really preferred the chaise lounge near it, and a big wing chair in the living room. Charley spent a few years with Bo before he died, but never would she lie on that chaise or chair. It was about six months after Bo was gone that she finally ventured there. Dogs know.

I grew up with Saint Bernards. I think my parents were in love with the idea of Nana, the motherly Newfoundland that looked after Wendy, Michael, and John, the three Darling children in *Peter Pan*, and decided since there were so many of us—nine, eventually—that only one Saint Bernard might not be enough to go around. Because of their great size and weight, there was no great inclination for them to jump up on our beds. During the summer they spent a lot of time in the river like big water buffalo barking at minnows or their shadows in the lapping tide. We cuddled with them and the youngest of us tried to ride them, but when they were wet and sandy, they sought a cool spot in the shade of the old gnarled mulberry trees that grew all over our land. My father loved those dogs and you could tell they had a special feeling for him. One of our originals, Saint, slept at his feet as he read in his favorite wing chair in the living room. One night Daddy got up, awakened by Saint's barking, and discovered the room was filled with smoke. He rushed out and discovered a fire blazing in the kitchen. He screamed out to my mother and all of us older children to grab the younger ones and crawl down the steps and out to safety. Later we realized Saint was not with us. He had returned to the burning house looking for my father. We lost her.

It's okay to sleep with your dog. Your dog is your mother, father, sister, brother, protector, and best friend.

To Geri Roper the message of this pillow could not be truer. "You know how they feel about you all the time," she sighs. "They ask for nothing in return except for a treat now and then and a teddy bear to love."

145

ambience

Creating mood with light, flickering
candles, a fireplace, scents from the
kitchen and garden, and the sound of
music from deft fingers on a piano
or from a stereo.

y mother-in-law Jean used to pick out a woman at a party and say to me, "She's got 'it'!" but what "it" encompassed was hard to define. It was an intangible quality or qualities that made her the woman every man wanted to be with and every woman wanted to be.

Some rooms have "it." The moment you step through the doorway there's a mood that envelops you like a warm embrace. Varying elements of light, color, texture, fragrance, heat, air, sound, and scale woo and exhilarate. Sometimes it's a grand public space whose soaring scale should intimidate but does not. I felt that way the first time I walked into the Duomo in Milan. So did Mark Twain as he recounted his experience in *The Innocents Abroad*: "What a wonder it is! So grand, so solemn, so vast! And yet so delicate, so airy, so graceful." Or sometimes it's a smaller, more personal space that feels bigger than life and timeless, like a small library filled with the warm smell of old leather books.

When I was growing up I was in charge of ambience. Possibly the task fell to me because, of the nine of us, I was most helpless in the kitchen and had a knack (along with others) for pulling a room together. To create a mood for rooms already burdened with the character of so many years of living was more of a supporting role for sure. My task was to garnish each, in summer, with cut herbs from the garden, and in winter, pewter pitchers filled with holly, bayberry, and branches of magnolia; to light candles tipped into tin chandeliers dangling from the dining room ceiling and in the wobbly silver and pewter candlestick holders scattered everywhere; to see that fires were crackling; and to ensure that Frank Sinatra crooned out a welcome as the first guest walked through the door.

Most of us don't have the advantage of living in an old house chock-full of inherent character and good bones. It is up to us to create it, and at special times to dust it with the magic of what my mother-in-law called "it" and most of us think of as ambience.

The Scent of a Home: From the Kitchen

I don't know if it's true, but I've heard that some coffee shops and bakeries actually entice customers through their doorways by piping out to the street the rich aroma of brewing coffee beans or chocolate chip cookies. Undoubtedly the marketers of those ubiquitous cinnamon buns for sale in every major airport are onto something. More times than not, I have been lured off track from my departure gate to follow the irresistible scent of those delectable squares of warm dough, pungent cinnamon, and piles of melting cream cheese frosting! Certainly Maureen Rodgers, proprietor of my favorite vintage bookstore nestled deep in the woods of upstate New York, is innocent of those "Mad Men" tactics! The scent of her homemade apple cider bubbling forth from a pot atop her little cast iron stove each winter seems as natural as the coziness she has created throughout her little wooden barn of books.

My sister Liza (Case History No. 6, page 161) has always had an unfair advantage in the olfactory/ambience department. Being a woman who loves to cook and lives to bake, the smells of her kitchen are legendary. On any given weekend, her friends in the neighborhood can step outside, sniff the air, and immediately say to themselves, Ah, yes, that Liza's at it again. Her kitchen is her studio for experimenting and creating every kind of food feat, so when friends arrive and head straight to the source, they are greeted by their aproned hostess—flour in her hair, icing on her cheek—and an irresistible symphony of scents created from tortes, tarts, cakes, pies, and batches of her trademark cookies, brownies, and blondies.

> "The moment you step through the doorway there's a mood that envelopes you like a warm embrace."

The Scent of a Home: From the Garden

Next to a cook's kitchen, a gardener's garden can help to set the mood of a home. When Oberto Gili entertains in Italy (see Case History No. 1, page 31) he can step outside to his own flower garden, but in New York, he has to go farther—either to the large wholesale flower district, which is "where you can get the best variety and the best prices" (a source for many of his photographic shoots) or in a pinch, to a small neighborhood food and flower market around the corner. He often buys roses for

Previous spread: Dripping with ambience are mismatched candles burning bright in an old candelabra.
Opposite: The smell of a just-baked pie or cookies in the oven warms up a house like a big cozy blanket.
Left: Liza Carter Norton, Case History No. 6, sets a table and quite a mood lighting up a dozen tapers stuck in old silver candleholders.

149

A kitchen counter lined with weathered cutting boards and little crocks of fragrant herbs straight from the garden.

their delicate color and fragrance. Rather than putting them in one big vase, he divides them into small bunches and sometimes creates a cluster of two or three on a table.

It is no surprise that a woman (Elena Salgueiro, Case History No. 4, page 105) who would have happily given up the entire exterior of her house to encroaching vines of wisteria until her husband finally had to chop a way into the blocked main entrance, would make a special point of always having fresh flowers, herbs, or branches from the garden on her table to create a mood for her guests.

Like Oberto and Elena, most of us would nominate flowers as the go-to, number-one element for creating an instant mood for any occasion, but how many of us would admit to using artificial flowers? When I visited the home of Natalie Gibson and Jon Wealleans (Case History No. 7, page 189) in London a few months back, my fake-flower guilt was transformed into pride. Right there blatantly and unabashedly center stage on the parlor's coffee table stood three vases filled with wildly realistic paper and plastic replicas of white lilies, pastel tulips, and stalwart stems of red amaryllis (see page 196) When I returned home to my large vase of artificial poppies prominently displayed in our living room, I felt newly vindicated. Though they will never be a substitute for the real thing, like the warmth of a real fire versus an electric one, they do add a spark of color when the real thing has wilted away.

Opposite: Wisteria pods and fragile roses entwined on the wrought iron balcony just outside of Elena Salgueiro's upstairs living room send the sweet scent of nature's offspring through a pair of French doors that are kept open most of the year.
Left: Oberto Gili, a city dweller, picks his favorite roses not from a garden but from a neighborhood market stand.

the magic of light

Candles

Growing up in a house built in the seventeenth century, first-time guests on an evening's visit might wonder, seeing candles lit everywhere and no lamps in sight, if we had electricity. We did, of course, but nothing, not even the most sophisticated electric candlelight bulb, could replicate the warm mood of a real dripping candle. We lit them in old tin chandeliers hanging from the ceilings, and stuck them in dozens of old silver and pewter candlestick holders protected by large glass hurricane lamps, in pierced tin lanterns, and in wall sconces everywhere. On a winter's night their glow and that from the logs burning in big open fireplaces created a mood that was cheering and comfortable.

No matter where you live, the moment you dim the lights and light a candle you are setting a mood that is instantly tangible. Dimmer switches are a must, as are bags of inexpensive votive candles. Because I light dozens of them displayed in collections of ironstone saucers, vintage custard cups, and little tin teacups borrowed from children's antique tea party sets, I prefer the unscented variety. In the summertime, I plop them into small clay flowerpots filled with sand. My sister Liza prefers tall creamy tapers elegantly shown off in mismatched old silver candlestick holders. Clustered together, they set a dazzling mood on a formal or informal dining room table (see hers on page 149).

 Candles Can Be Drips:
To protect your furniture from the inevitable dripping candle wax, invest in the dripless variety, but be forewarned that almost all candles are potential drippers. If you can't live with that, try those clever little candle collars that act as a kind of safety net for those waxy rivers.

 Candle Scrapes:
One of the best tools for scraping up old candle wax on a table's surface is a rubber spatula. Knives, even dull ones, can scrape up as much of the table's finish as wax. Just nudge the spatula's edge gently, a little bit at a time.

 Color:
I always preferred the purity of white or cream candles until one Thanksgiving when my husband presented me with a bagful that looked like oversized Crayolas. Doubtful at first, I have now come to prefer them. I display them together in a candlelabra or chandelier letting the colors play off one another. They have a cheerful quality all year-round, but especially in the colder months (see for yourself on page 147).

Candlelight is an incredible mood enhancer, but it is a lot of trouble and potentially dangerous. Keep a close watch on where you place your candles, keeping them far away from textiles and flammable objects. When possible protect them with hurricane lanterns and always keep a careful watch over them.

Lamps

Although Oberto Gili is a big lover of candles, he sometimes isn't up to the effort. At those times he relies on the spots of light created by the collection of contemporary and vintage lamps dotted throughout his apartment. A pair of modern lamps creates soft spots on his primary work and entertaining table (as seen on pages 36–37). He loves that he can raise, lower, and swivel them around to create just the right spotlight on food or flowers.

Just like candles, lamps can create mood and softness. The tints of the bulbs and the colors of the shades create intimate patches of light. If you want to create a mood with lamplight, use your dimmer or exchange your bulbs for ones that are a lower wattage and even a softer color. You can also consider dressing up your lamps for a special party by changing the lampshades. Or, like our Case History No. 3, page 77, take a chance and do something different. It was the week before Christmas and, lacking a chandelier for the ceiling of her new house, Pamela Bell pinch-hit with a bouquet of branches strung with little white lights. It hit a welcoming home run the night she and her three children moved in and three years later it is still there.

Opposite: Instead of tea, a doll's collection of teacups serves up flickering tea-light candles.
Left: An impromptu twig chandelier strung with little white lights brings a spirit of fun and festivity to Pamela Bell's more formal plaster-carved living room ceiling.

155

How to Survive Without a Fireplace

When my husband and I were searching for a getaway from the city, we found the perfect one until I discovered its fatal flaw—no fireplace! It's one thing to live in a city apartment without a fireplace, but a country house without a fireplace is anathema. When the owner saw something had gone drastically wrong, I confessed the house's curse. And to our great surprise, he replied, "No problem, we'll build one." And he did, and we spent many a cozy night in front of it. Though this is a true story, it may be a little frustrating since not many landlords would agree to build a fireplace. More than anything, it serves to represent how strongly (obsessed) I am about the healing power of sitting in front of an open fire and the pleasure I believe it offers every guest invited to share its warmth. Fires add charm to the most boring rooms. There is the physical warmth of the burning wood, its smell, and the cheery glow cast over every piece of furniture in the room. To get the most mood out of a fire, keep your lights low and your candles bright. And the most romantic thing of all is to serve dinner in front of it.

How to live without a fireplace? A legitimate alternative is the gas-log fireplace. They have come a long way aesthetically. If gas is out of the question, there are some deceptively clever plug-in fireplaces that resemble cast iron stoves. They won't warm up your tootsies, but they might provide a hint of charming fakery, like my paper poppies. If all else fails, bring on the candles!

Right: A triple dose of warmer-uppers—homemade stew, just-baked bread, and a cozy place in front of the fire.
Opposite: Gas logs, though efficient, will never replace the genuine warmth, the smell, and the sounds of a crackling wood fire.

sound

Music

Think of all the movies you've ever loved, and then think of them without the music that invisibly knitted each scene together, creating moods of mystery, seduction, joy, adventure, fear, harmony, and triumph. During my many years working alongside the photographer Bruce Weber, I always admired the two important pieces of equipment that had to be on set no matter where we were shooting: a large CD player and an even larger box of CDs. Before he took one shot, Bruce would confer with all of us and the subjects he was about to shoot to pick a song or symphony they would like to hear that would help to create a mood. It was a little like scoring a movie. And wouldn't all of us love our daily lives to be scored like that? So many people today are walking around plugged into their own portable soundtracks, so this appears to have happened. We travel to work with music, work out with music, write to music, get our teeth cleaned to music, fall in love to music, and, of course, entertain with music.

Music is the salt and pepper of an evening. It adds a dash of something to buoy our spirits, and make us dance, laugh, feel nostalgic and seductive or, as Judy Garland belted out, "Forget your troubles, come on get happy . . ." Music can do that. So along with setting the table, lighting the candles, building a fire, and arranging the flowers, we choose a certain kind of music to enhance the feeling we have attempted to create in our home.

There are so many devices that have been used to pipe music throughout our homes.

When we were children it was an old phonograph hidden in the bottom of a large wooden cupboard off the dining room. Stacks of our favorite LPs (that is long-playing records, for those of you too young to know!) were stored nearby. On those special occasions when we entertained lots of friends and family, we took turns playing DJ and spinning our favorite tunes, from the Rolling Stones to Elvis and Frank Sinatra. Today the old "stereo" has been replaced by our children's lineup of iPods loaded with their favorite songs.

The other night upon my arrival at a friend's apartment for dinner, there was a wonderful, unconventional piece of music playing. It turned out to be Phillip Glass music called "Glass Reflections" by the Cello Octet Conjunto Iberico. Though the apartment had a mood that was intelligent and slightly bohemian, it was the music that lured me in and stayed with me throughout the night. And music isn't the only kind of desirable sound. In the atelier of Nathalie Lété (Case History No. 2, page 61) outside of Paris, the music comes from a group of twittering songbirds that live in a roomy cage propped on a sunny ledge next to windows (see pages 66–67) reflecting the trees and sky outside. "I need birds and their songs in my studio otherwise I feel lonely in this big space," she says.

Music in our homes, whether live or electronic, has the same joyous effect of lifting our spirits and making us merry. Listen carefully and you will hear the sound of Bach's "Little Preludes" being played by an ardent twelve-year-old pianist, Ksenia Salgueiro.

living with food

case history no. 6 **liza carter norton**

How a passionate chef cooked up the perfect kitchen and found a recipe for organizing the flying flour, rolling pins, cake molds, whisks, and pie tins, as well as her extensive collection of cookbooks and magazines.

liza

Born in: Virginia
Family: her husband John, and their grown children Mary Randolph and John Tyler
Home: Westchester, New York
Lived there: thirteen years
Description: a mid-nineteenth-century gambrel-roofed caretaker's house last added on to in the thirties
Challenges: to create a high-tech, efficient, cozy kitchen to support her huge passion for cooking and baking, and to find a way to keep it organized
Most hated chore: laundry and cleaning
Favorite thing about your house:
That it always makes me happy when I come home
A Perfect House? It's like a love affair. I give it time and energy and love and in return it's a haven for me, my family, and my friends.

Previous spread: A tower of old and new baking tins for cakes, pies, tarts, breads, cupcakes, and muffins awaits a marathon baking session.
This page (clockwise from top): Liza recently earned her cooking wings (and chef's toque) with a degree in pastry arts from the French Culinary Institute; straight from her oven—a pear torte; Liza's collections of antique linens and dessert plates are only rivaled by her collection of vintage paintings.
Opposite: The joy of cooking creates the burden of a sink full of dirty dishes, which even modern technology cannot eliminate.

t's probably not a wise thing to make your sister a case history in a book on the touchy subject of how we live perfectly and imperfectly, but she seemed curious and willing to share how she, the sixth child in our family, has always been our "top chef" and somehow could manage to make six cakes or twenty-four chocolate-covered Easter eggs before breakfast. While her friends were reading their favorite girlhood writers and swooning over Mick Jagger and the Beatles, she was devouring cookbooks, cooking magazines (see her archival stacks on page 174) or anything she could get her hands on about food. She attributes the cookbook passion to our grandmother Ga-Ga, who Liza says, "read cookbooks like novels. She would read a recipe and taste the ingredients in her head, smacking her lips with a barely audible 'that tastes good!'"

The early roots of this love of food was probably cooked up right in the family kitchen. "I started baking," she recalls, "because we had so many birthdays to take care of and both our parents worked." Her first birthday cake for one of us was "a hit," and that was the beginning of what we still call "Liza Cakes," which now include not only birthday cakes, but all manner of baked goods—pies and cookies and tarts—and now as family members have grown up, wedding cakes. Another inspiration grew right outside the kitchen window—an herb garden designed by our father and based on those of Thomas Jefferson at Monticello. It was there beside our father and mother that she became a gardener. They planted over 150 different herbs. "Mother would send me or another sister or brother out to pick herbs for a meal, letting us decide what would go in the herb butter or sauce or would be sprinkled in a salad." When she was twelve she got a summer job at a small yacht club with a popular dining room. She was the "B&C" for the husband and wife team (friends of the family) who had retired from Rochester, New York to run it. It was only later that she found out that B& C stood for "beck and call!" And that she was—doing all sorts of things, including reviewing the food inventory in the top of a very hot attic. Ultimately she credits the pair with teaching her to be more open in her thinking about ingredients, like turning what we thought were disgusting sugar toads into an exotic fish salad.

Some years later, after picking up a college degree in art, her other passion, she moved to New York City and lived for a time with me, my husband, and our two children. It wasn't long before she was off on her own designing textiles for some of the biggest names in the business and traveling the world in search of unusual resources and unusual taste sensations. The zeal for cooking, baking, and, after she married John Norton, for entertaining was never thwarted by the limited space of a tiny city kitchen. Her dream was to one day have a kitchen like the one she grew up in and a garden, too. That dream was realized thirteen years ago when she and her family moved from the city to an old mid-nineteenth-century

Opposite: Liza's ready to roll with a good old rolling pin, newly kneaded dough for bread, and all kinds of pie crusts.
Left: Liza's cooking passion started with family birthday cakes.

gambrel-roofed house that had been part of a larger estate in the countryside of Westchester County. It needed a new roof and windows—big picture things that they slowly took care of—so her big dream of the kitchen with a fireplace (like the one she had grown up in) with a huge marble-topped worktable for baking, had to wait.

In the meantime she had no trouble filling up the house she saw as having "too many walls to cover and rooms full of bookcases yearning for books and tchotchkes" with chairs (sixty-two at her husband's last count), eleven benches, sofas, pillows to cozy-up window seats, old textiles inspired by our mother's collection of beautifully embroidered bed linens that we never slept on ("too wrinkled and who was going to iron them?" she questioned), and boxes of antique prints (birds and botanicals) inspired by our father's love of antique maps. Her collections for cooking and entertaining—platters, dessert sets, tea sets, at least fifteen sets of antique china, silver table settings, table linens, silver candlesticks, cookbooks, baking molds, and baking tins awaited their eventual home in her dream kitchen.

On a sunny winter morning, a glowing fire (provided by a click of a switch—gas logs are just easier and cleaner, Liza hates to admit) adds to the warmth of her favorite spot for a hasty cup of coffee before big baking projects are underway on her marble-topped island—the stage for many a winning performance.

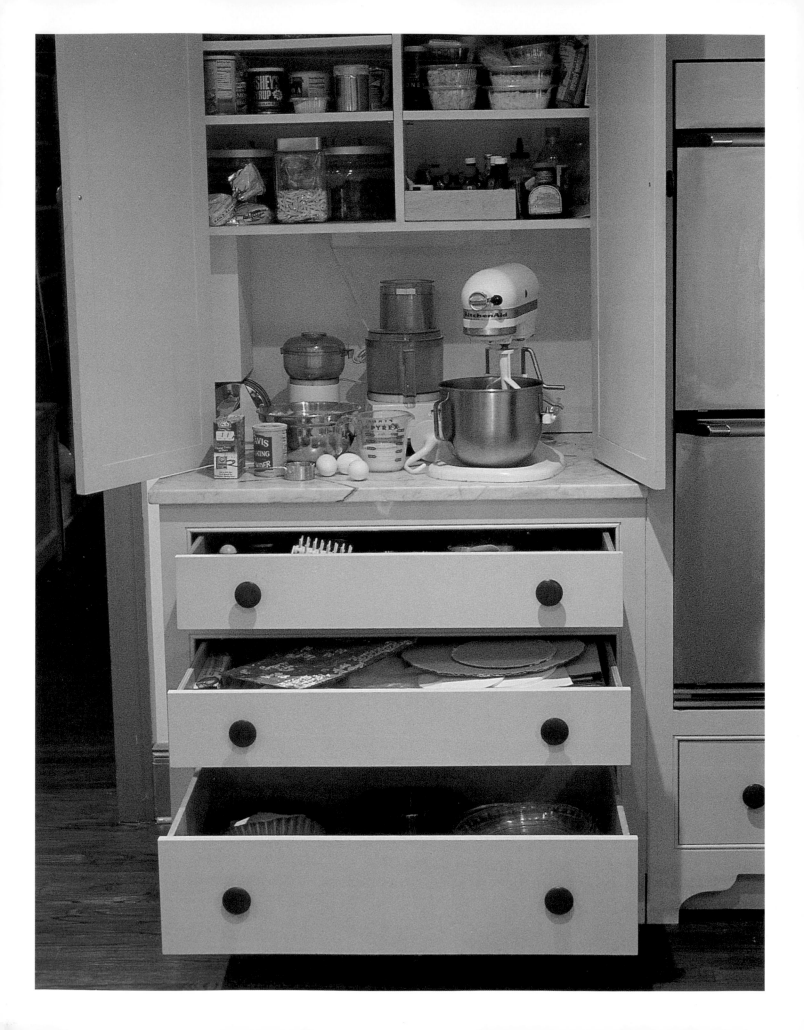

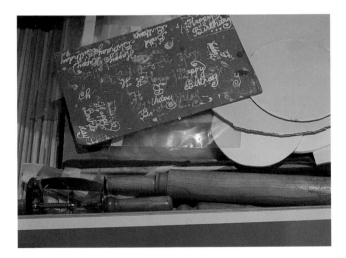

Liza's Baking Cupboard

One of the things you get to do when you're both the dreamer and architect of your fantasy kitchen is to build in the things you were always missing and always wanted. In Liza's case it was a special cabinet to store all the ingredients and tools of her baking obsession. She modeled it after a cupboard in our mother's kitchen that had two large doors that could hide in a flash a cooked-up mess. To keep hers handy she placed it next to the wall of ovens to the right.

On the marble counter (opposite) are her KitchenAid, Cuisinart, small food processors, and blender. Housed in the shelves above are nuts, chocolate, dried fruits, and vanilla extract. The three big drawers below organize everything else.

The top drawer (this page, top) has everything for baking: cutters, decorating tips, pie dishes, and more. To keep it from sliding into chaos, she created a grid out of separate wooden boxes.

The middle drawer (this page, center) contains boxes of parchment paper, rolling pins, and some exercises in cake writing.

The bottom drawer (this page, bottom) stores her favorite collection of pie plates and molds. She keeps a hidden stash of her most-used cookbooks in a compartment at the bottom of her prepping island (not pictured). The rest are archived in her special cook's library, seen on page 173.

"Let them eat cake!" does not have the same meaning when uttered by Liza! With eight cake layers just out of the oven, a pear torte and an apple pie in the works, and mounds of icing standing by, her order is music to all who hear it.

during their sixth year in the house, the original kitchen, which had been only nine by eight feet, was opened up and combined with two other little rooms—an eating area and a no-man's-land kind of hallway—to create a breathtakingly beautiful, light-filled space measuring eighteen by twenty-six feet. It was transformed into "the Hub." With a fireplace, stuffed chairs, an upholstered bench, and an old Welsh cupboard crammed with Liza's eclectic pottery, porcelain, and majolica sitting right opposite her long-awaited marble-topped table/island/bar, it's certainly the place to be anytime, but particularly when my sister is stirring up something for company. This could be neighborhood friends, son John's swim team or singing club, daughter M.R.'s post-play-rehearsal gathering of hungry thespians, or Thanksgiving dinner for forty. When Liza's in the kitchen it's standing-room-only. Her cooking island becomes her stage for a meal, a dessert, a three tiered cake-in-progress. She's stirring and tasting and whipping and peeling and icing and chatting and dancing, and enjoying every minute of her two favorite things: cooking and entertaining. Her love of food, she clearly states, goes back to the success of her first family birthday cake, "the pleasure that comes from people enjoying it." And not just her cooking, but her home. "If you don't care about how people feel in your home you should meet them at a restaurant!" she exclaims.

Now that she's got her dream kitchen, three ovens, the perfect baking cabinet, and lots of counter space, is she perfectly organized? Well, not exactly. Her husband calls it her "overdoing it" streak. "There's that crucial moment," she confesses, "when everything's done, in its place, and there's another hour to go before guests arrive and I say to myself, I have time, there must be something else I can bake." And, then, just when she thinks she is ready, the cooking chaos begins again; as friends pour in through the kitchen door, so does the fun!

Perhaps in a large family everyone is looking for their niche. My sister found hers very early, and it has stuck. Though her kitchen today is far from the one where her training began, her thoughts are not. She returns to it often with her portable cook's tool case and notebooks filled with her favorite recipes, including Ga-Ga's. All of us—her family and biggest fans—await the smells of her cooking: Ga-Ga's cheese biscuits in the oven, mother's Brunswick stew bubbling on top, and a cooling chocolate "Nancy" Cake to bring us all home again.

Right: When she was six, Liza's daughter Mary Randolph took it upon herself to embellish the pages of her mother's recipe diary with charming crayon drawings.
Opposite: When the chef is off duty you'll find her in her cozy little study above the kitchen bent over her antique desk writing up recipes, or on the floor paging through stacks of cooking and food books from her eclectic library.

Scalloped Potatoes Mean "I Love You!"

One of my sister's favorite food stories is about the night years ago when she was preparing dinner for a bunch of friends in her tiny six-by-six-foot kitchen and one of them "who particularly loved my cooking," came into the kitchen to see what was going on.

He: "You're making scalloped potatoes?"
She: "Yes! Is that okay?"
He: "Look, if you just invited me for dinner because you had to, you'd cook a baked potato. If you liked me, you'd make mashed potatoes. But if you really loved me, you'd make scalloped potatoes!"
She: "I guess I love you!"

The moral of the story: "That's when I learned for real that cooking is about that 'labor of love!' It's what you put into a meal, that extra effort people really appreciate. So for me, cooking for others has always been a love fest and feast!"

Opposite: After an avalanche of her collected food magazines threatened to destroy her upstairs study (and her marriage!) they were promptly exiled to the garage where they teeter precariously against bags of fertilizer and garden bric-a-brac.
Top: A handwritten page from one of Liza's personal recipe journals.
Bottom: A collection of vintage cookbooks from the forties.

entertaining

Making room in our homes and often
our kitchens for a welcome informality,
a new kind of hospitality, and a pinch
of madness.

in the kitchen

What would Charles Dickens have thought seeing family and friends gathered in our kitchen sipping wine, shucking corn, snipping at the ends of fresh green beans, and slicing up juicy tomatoes and creamy mozzarella? No doubt he would have raised an eyebrow at such a scene, having set many a droll episode of his own in the mean and merry kitchens of nineteenth-century England. But even in Dickens's world there were boundaries. The kitchen was a place for cooks and servants, not the host and hostess and their guests. In my grandmother's time, in the fifties, it wasn't that different. Ga-Ga, as we called her, had a large, airy kitchen with an attached breakfast nook where she shared informal meals with my grandfather, Pop, and her visiting grandchildren, but guests did not dare push the heavy swinging door that led into her inner sanctum! It wasn't until the last couple of decades that doors and walls finally came tumbling down and the kitchen was liberated by cooks (both women and men) who had long tired of being isolated in the scullery. Architects, at the urging of clients who wanted to live more openly, reconfigured the house with the kitchen at its center. It became the live-action amphitheater for guests to spectate or participate in the preparation of the meal itself.

Based on my imperfect poll of the case histories in this book, all agree the kitchen is where everyone wants to be. Whether spacious or tiny; cluttered or clean; in the country, city, or suburbs; in the U.S. or U.K., or in Italy or France, the kitchen is unquestionably the heart of our homes.

Our kitchen in our New York City apartment is far from an amphitheater, and yet its smallness (eight by eight feet of actual people space) does not deter our guests from piling in. Its location—right off the front door—contributes to that, as does the smell of whatever's cooking in the oven and the fun of being part of a chummy kind of chaos.

My sister Liza Carter Norton (Case History No. 6, page 161) gave up a kitchen like that when she and her family left the city thirteen years ago for a house in Westchester County. What they didn't give up was the coziness. Guests still crowd into their new, generously proportioned kitchen (see pages 170–171), leaning on the marble-topped center island as if it were a friendly old bar in an English pub. When Geri Roper (Case History No. 5, page 133) extended her house, a former barn in rural New Jersey, it was to accommodate her family, friends, and lots of dogs in a big open-air kitchen with a fireplace and lots of lounging space near all the cooking activity. Elena Salgueiro (Case History No. 4, page 105) moved her penned-in kitchen at her home in Thomery, France, from the first floor to what had been a garage beneath. Her new space provides room for a large dining table and open access to a comfortable family room—a perfect staging area for her four children's plays and projects, and just within earshot while she's stirring up something delicious as an encore. Natalie Gibson's story (Case History No. 7, page 189) is the same. No matter how hard she tries to encourage her guests to have a drink in the comfy front parlor of one of the oldest houses in London, they all seem to end up in a kitchen that was space-challenged way before she moved in some forty years ago and now leaves little room (thanks to her accumulation of treasures) for cooking and/or friends!

All of us who have opted, by choice or not, to cook and entertain in this open-kitchen atmosphere have found (hopefully) ways to deal with what it dishes out through different kinds of improvisation. I love people in our kitchen, but since I have little space to serve I cover the sink with a large wooden cutting board and pile my mismatched plates, crocks of silverware, and all manner of red and white checked napkins I've collected for years, right there. To keep hot foods hot, I let people help themselves right from the pots on the stovetop and arrange the salad, bread, and room-temperature fare on the center table and two small counters nearby. There is no formal seating, so guests improvise, spread out through the apartment, eating out of their laps or on makeshift tables of books piled on the floor and on tables everywhere. When chairs run out, I pull out my stackable café chairs; it's a little like alfresco dining inside. Since people eat at different paces and there is no more room in the kitchen to serve desert, I set it up on a long, narrow trestle table in the outer hallway. I plunk down homemade pies and cookies (usually contributed by my baking friends) and a big bowl of ice cream. When I discover we haven't enough clean silverware, I quickly remove the temporary cutting board that's hiding the sink to do

a last-minute rinse-off. Last Thanksgiving, with thirty-five to feed, I gave up on that and pulled out my backup stash of plastic forks. Another idea is to consider a plateless dessert of cookies and brownies or ice cream cones and Klondike Bars that require only a pile of extra-large paper napkins.

My sister Liza, who has an "overdoing it" streak (according to her husband) would never hear of such a thing. She can't restrain herself to one heavenly homemade chocolate layer cake but must offer at least three others, in case someone might prefer her incredible banana cake with caramel icing or a stack of still-warm brownies or blondies. Though she often sets up her meal buffet style right in the kitchen, multitasking her marble-topped island, sometimes she sets up her battalions of desserts on her more formal dining room table amid legions of flickering candles. Oberto Gili (Case History No. 1, page 31) prefers more intimate dinner parties in the long, open ground-floor space of his New York City brownstone, accommodating cooking, living, and working all in one. He carries his platters of homemade pasta to his guests seated at one of several tables he has effortlessly transformed with candlelight and flowers from a place for work to a place for pleasure.

Previous spread: A kitchen cupboard fully loaded with stacks of durable ironstone dishes and food staples is ready for any entertaining challenge.

Hospitality

Memories carry me back (just like the song we sang as children) to old Virginia, and the tradition of hospitality that part of the world is known for. I grew up in the heart of what is known as "southern hospitality," country, but I don't think I knew what it was until I left it behind. Both my parents were born in Richmond, Virginia, as was I, my six sisters, and two brothers. Until I was ten, we lived on Monument Avenue under the watchful eye of General Robert E. Lee astride his beloved horse Traveller. I shared those years in that big brick house with two families: My mother's family lived on the upper floors. This included her father, her two aunts (my grandfather's sisters, who raised her after the untimely death of her mother), and one of her two sisters. Our family—my parents and five of us children (at that time)—lived on the ground floor. Though we had two distinct households—two kitchens, two dining rooms, two living rooms, and separate dens, bedrooms, and bathrooms—we shared one home and an abundance of love. The house was always full of people, mostly family—those who lived there and those who constantly visited from near and far—and always friends dropping by "to pay their respects" to my great-aunts and my grandfather, who were from a long line of Virginians and well thought of in the community. I remember a little silver tray on a table in their hallway that collected the personal calling cards of these visitors. Though reserved mainly for formal visits during illnesses or a death, I

think it was second nature to most of my great-aunts' lady friends to carry a supply of them in a special little case along with their fans and smelling salts.

During our holiday "open house" celebrations, my grandfather's dining room table and ours were laid with thick white linen tablecloths and set with all the best silver serving pieces that offered up, buffet style, the favorite family recipes prepared in both of our kitchens and shared along with many other dishes brought by our friends. A typical menu included Smithfield ham, homemade biscuits, turnip greens, rice, thick brown gravy, sweet potato pudding, tomato aspic, Brunswick Stew, panned oysters, big silver bowls of homemade egg nog laced with bourbon, rum and brandy, salted Virginia peanuts, cheese biscuits, peach upside-down cake, and jam cake. It was those early gatherings that instilled in us some enduring lessons about making a house a home to guests. We learned that the fun of socializing was not just sharing food and drink, but also telling stories, and singing and dancing, and not only with one another but with people of all ages. We also learned the important lesson of waiting to serve ourselves only after the guests had helped themselves. In later years a family alert—"FHB"—was whispered among us kids; it meant family hold back!

An old wooden worktable in our country kitchen surrounded by a generous-sized bench and an endless supply of mismatched chairs that easily accommodates last-minute guests. The same goes for the plate rack behind it, which makes grabbing an extra dish just as easy.

181

At Home

● **Pull out all the stops when entertaining.** If you have the space for formal entertaining, don't think of Thanksgiving as the only event for which you set your table with your finest table linens, silver, and china.

● **Personalize your table.** For a larger gathering, handwritten place cards on the dining table add such a personal touch and make your guests feel more appreciated. It also gives you the opportunity to break up couples and old friends to sit with dining partners they may not know. This will add an element of conviviality to the evening and make it more exciting.

● **Introduce your guests.** Make sure you take time to introduce any arriving guests, particularly people who are newcomers. I usually put the bar at the far end of our living room so guests have to pass through the crowd and meet and greet everyone on their way to a glass of spirits.

● **Make room.** Though I think most people like to be a little cozy in social situations, sometimes it's nice to have a place where they can escape for a private chat. On occasions when large crowds were coming to our apartment, I actually set up a little bar in our bedroom. Guests kind of love the informality of that, even if it means sitting on a bed piled with coats.

● **Check your coat.** Entertaining a crowd in coat season can be a bit of a challenge, especially in an apartment. Years ago I invested in a fold-up rolling rack that we store under our bed and place out in the hall (with our neighbors' permission) when guests are expected. At the end of the evening neither hosts nor guests have to spend a minute searching for coats under a mountain of them.

At a Friend's Home

● **Play the hospitality card.** Instead of a business card, create your own personalized calling cards to attach to your host/hostess gift of flowers, a bottle of wine, or better yet, a favorite homemade dish. As a surprise thank-you attach the card (when they're not looking) to their refrigerator door with a cute magnet!

● **Win the most valuable guest award.** Good friends make good guests. When you can help your host and hostess, jump in! That doesn't mean take over or get in the way, just simply ask, "How can I help?"

Unlock those velvet-lined silver chests and liberate your finest silverware. Share your best with your guests on even the least formal occasion.

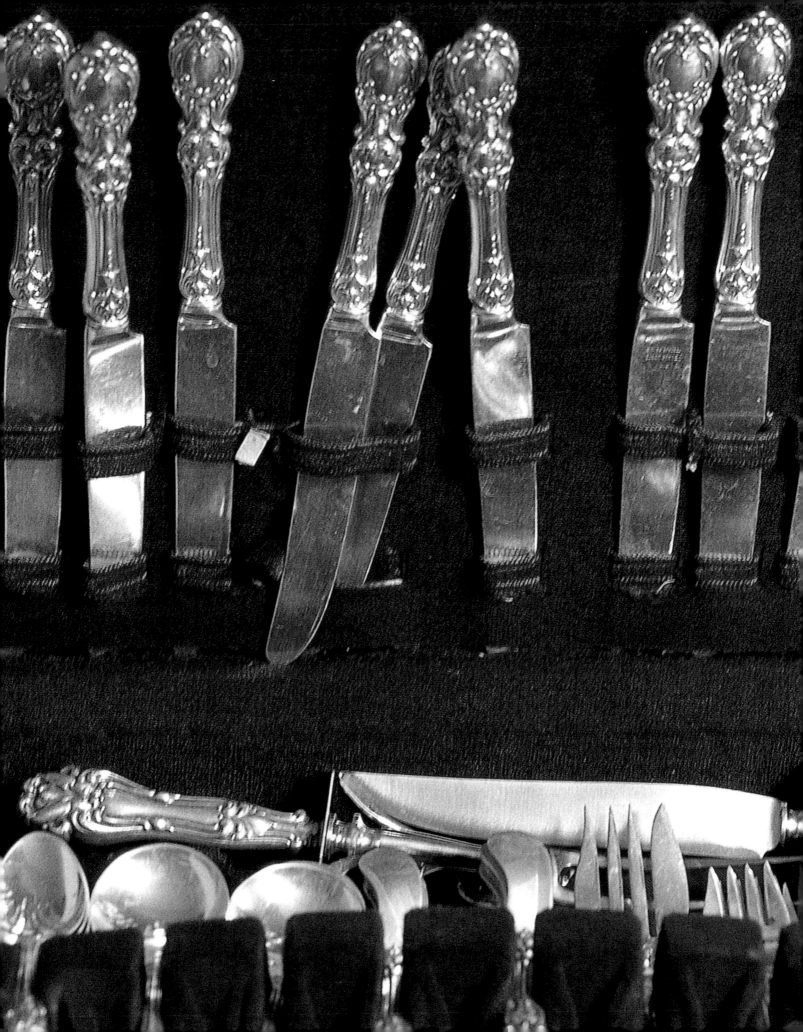

My childhood memories of southern hospitality conjure up candlelit tables, pewter bowls of Brunswick stew, a side dish of barbecue, and fresh-from-the-oven homemade rolls.

the party's over

I have to admit that though paper plates for a large dinner party are certainly acceptable, even desirable, particularly when dinner's over and things start to crash and burn in the kitchen, I still love to serve on china. For a large crowd I cobble together a stack that's mismatched but serves the purpose. I feel the same way about paper napkins. Even if none of them match, I always prefer cloth. Glasses are a huge challenge. Because people put them down at a party and can never find them, you must have at least twice as many glasses as guests. And though I believe in serving wine in real wine glasses, I always have a backup supply of plastic ones. Speaking of which, plastic milk crates, an inexpensive purchase at any of those home storage meccas, are handy receptacles (if you lack counter space) for all those used glasses, plates, and silverware.

After the last guest has gone (except for those good souls who have volunteered for cleanup duty) many party-givers are ready to give it up and collapse into the nearest chair or bed. Liza Carter Norton puts it this way: "I start off neat and organized, but by the end of the evening, with plates, glasses, and napkins from the cocktail hour; platters, bowls, dinner plates, more napkins, and more glasses; and dessert plates and silver galore from dinner—oh, my, I'm not in Kansas anymore!" This post-party terrain is not a pretty picture, but most of us would prefer to push on through rather than face it in the morning.

I patrol the aftermath with a big plastic bucket to catch leftover beer and wine from bottles and glasses. Beside me is my husband armed with a large, heavy-duty garbage bag to scoop up the empty bottles, used cocktail napkins, and all other trash-bound debris. After cleanup is organized, we load up the dishwasher while reviewing the night—the guests, the food, what we will and won't forget—we take one more look around to make sure all candles have been blown out, and then, at last, it's into bed.

Perfect Party Ingredient: A Pinch of Madness

According to Marie-Hélène de Rothschild ". . . those who are small in spirit, who are mean, narrow-minded or timid, should leave entertaining to others. For however rich or poor one is, certain ingredients are essential: a pinch of madness, two dashes of refinement, three grains of effort—and a few heartbeats . . . or as they would say, *mettre les petits plats dans les grands.*"

I never came close to being invited to one of Marie-Hélène de Rothschild's legendary balls held at the Hotel Lambert, her exquisite Paris residence on the Ile Saint Louis or at the Château de Ferrieres, the childhood home of her husband Guy de Rothschild, but if I had been I'm sure I would have a great time. La Barone, as she was known, certainly knew how to throw a heck of a party. In an article about one given in Paris in 1992, Suzy Menkes, the fashion editor of *The International Herald Tribune,* dubbed La Barone "Society's Star Choreographer." La Barone knew how to invite the right people and how to mix them up. Her eclectic guest list was chosen carefully from the crème de la crème of international society, politics, royalty, fashion, and film. She was reportedly not only the social queen of Paris, but the ultimate perfectionist. In the aforementioned article, she shared with Suzy Menkes some of her trade secrets. "A party starts," she said, "with the invitation, which is designed 'to inspire people.'" For her surrealist ball in 1972, the invitation was printed back to front on a backdrop of René Magritte clouds so that it had to be deciphered with a mirror. The next step, she reported to Menkes, was to plan an arresting entrance, like the Alice-through-the-looking-glass mirrored entrance complete with costumed white rabbits at the Hotel Lambert for her 1987 Bal des Fees. De Rothschild died in 1996 and to this day people write and talk about her parties and her "persnickety perfectionism," as Menkes wrote. One tale reports her demand that scrambled eggs for four hundred be rescrambled since they weren't the perfect yellow. Though most of us won't be throwing balls like La Barone, her instincts about entertaining were top-notch. The best for me is from her recipe for entertaining—"a pinch of madness, two dashes of refinement, three grains of effort and a few heartbeats . . ." I take her "pinch of madness" to mean depart from the ordinary: Create an environment in your home that induces your guests to depart from their ordinary selves. Candlelight can do that; so can music. Flowers or a table set in an unusual way can as well.

At one recent Christmas, my sister Nell and I were challenged to find seating for forty at Muskettoe Pointe Farm. At the last minute we carried in from the outside a seventeen-foot trestle table my parents had once built for a wedding-rehearsal dinner. We set it up in the front hall, a part of the house we have never eaten in, and lined the center of the table with a dozen mismatched candlesticks. For seating we brought in picnic benches from the garden and camouflaged their seats with gingham fabric. Everyone wanted to sit at that table! It was out of the ordinary—our pinch of madness.

One pinch of madness that always makes a party much more fun is including free-spirited children.

living with Obsession

case history no. 7 **natalie gibson**

The updated tale of the woman who
lived in a shoe, with the shoe being
a tall, skinny, four-hundred-year-old
house in London, home to many cats
(eight) and too many treasures.

natalie

Born in: London, brought up in northern Scotland
Family: her husband Jon Wealleans, two grown sons, Hoot and Brodie, and eight cats
Home: London
Lived there: forty-seven years
Description: a four-hundred-year-old, three-story brick row house near Tower Bridge with a small garden in the back
Challenges: to fit it all in and still have room for the boys (thank goodness they've moved out!), her textile design, Jon's painting, cooking, brave friends, and of course, the cats
Solutions: push it to one side, work on the floor, don't worry, be happy
Words to live by: from Jon, as I'm heading out to a market, "Please don't buy anymore junk!"
A Perfectly Kept House? I don't collect, really, things just sort of pile up

Previous spread: With the exception of a mismatched collection of cups and teapots, Natalie Gibson's jam-packed cupboard defies what one might expect to find in a proper English pantry.
This page (clockwise from top): Natalie and her husband at the doorway of their home; attempting to keep junk mail at bay, Jon has taped a warning on the mail slot; just inside, Natalie's pink coat and finery are a precursor of things to come.
Opposite: Hail to Pansy Puff Ball, the only real cat in the photograph (sent as a Christmas card), reigning over a tumult of kitchen tools and cooking paraphernalia.

here kitty, kitty, kitty!" is something you might not want to utter in this old London row house. If you do, be prepared for a possible stampede of paws, whiskers, black, white, and orange fur, glinting cat eyes, and rows of sharp little white teeth from the eight cats on the premises: Cool Dude, Pansy Puff Ball, Helpless, Katmandu, Blondie, Ziggy (scaredy-cat), Angus, and Priscilla Queen of the Desert. Natalie Gibson and Jon Wealleans know better than that. No. 9 has been their home for over four decades, and in that time the home of as many as twelve cats, two macaws, a parrot, and, lest we forget, sons Hoot and Brodie, who said their goodbyes long ago (they're grown) to the cats, the birds, and all the stuff their mom ("Blame her, not Dad") packed into the three stories, plus a basement, of the charming old brick row house, circa 1650, in the area known as Bermondsy in London.

Among the lively and curious things piled and scattered around three large vases of paper flowers on a coffee table in the front parlor (see page 196), is a book celebrating the fashion prints of London's swinging sixties. Inside is the work of a young textile designer named Natalie Gibson. Though she started her career in painting at the Chelsea Art School, she later switched to textile design at the Royal College of Art. In between design projects like special fashion prints for the style icon Twiggy, she supported herself with teaching stints at London's top fashion schools. Since 1981, she has directed the Fashion Prints department at the prestigious Central St. Martins, sharing her passion with the likes of former students Stella McCartney, Alexander McQueen, and John Galliano. Along the way she met Jon Wealleans, an architect with a more cleaned-up, modernist aesthetic, but with an offbeat affection for the work of Frank Lloyd Wright, Charles Rennie Mackintosh, and, for the last eight years, as an artist, of his wife's household collections. "He's jolly lucky to have my stuff!" Natalie proclaims. In the catalog to his current exhibition, "Kitchen Kitsch," she reports her friends' outrage at reading that "he combs markets and collects things . . ." "Excuse me!" she puts in, "Jon has always hated all my junk." (For his point of view, see page 202.) Nonetheless, their affection for each other (and the cats) has certainly overcome any hardships engendered by living with it. "I don't collect really," she insists, "I am helplessly attracted to certain things and they just sort of pile up!" Like all the cat stuff—stalking, pouncing; sitting pretty on dresser tops, cupboard shelves, and window ledges; woven into rugs, printed on pillows, painted and replicated on all manner of things, including meowing magnets on the refrigerator's yellow door. Memphis, their big blue and yellow macaw, and a little parrot Phoebe, seem to have motivated a feathered collection that has conquered every available perching place, particularly in the kitchen. "Whenever friends see a cat or parrot object they feel obliged to get it for me." Clearly she does not have the the heart to say no. After their sons Hoot and Brodie moved

Opposite: Lurking inside the wisteria-framed kitchen window, a marble-eyed chat epouvantail (meant to hang in cherry trees to scare away birds) spies three (of the eight) real-life felines who inhabit the premises. Left: Katmandu, Pansy Puff Ball, and Helpless sitting pretty on a garden bench.

Natalie Gibson, not Sheena, is the queen of this wildly colored jungle of a kitchen where exotic parrots fly and perch, and outnumbered cats stalk through the pink and turquoise terrain of pots and pans, whisks, wooden spoons, teacups, pots, and everyday crockery.

"I don't really collect, I'm attracted to certain things, I get them, and they accumulate."

—Natalie

out, two rooms freed up. Jon took one as his studio and the other was designated as a guest room with the caveat that in between visitors, Natalie could store the overflow of wildly colored clothes and accessories that tend to match her raspberry locks. "I avoid beige," she says quite matter of factly. "I don't wear a lot of black. I think I'm just a magpie. I love color—bright pink and red, turquoise and blue, and patterns and lots of roses." This sums up the palette of the guest room, as well as the entire house, starting with the Moroccan blue of the front door and the shutters with carved-out hearts.

Caring for all this stuff is not a problem. "I absolutely hate cleaning. I hate Hoovering! I like cleaning little corners. It makes such a huge difference, but the idea of doing it again is too much."

With two artists in the house, there is the additional challenge of what to do with the tools of their trade. Jon's studio, lined with bookshelves, a drawing board, a mobile tower of drawers, his easel, and nearby worktable set up a like a still life of palette, paint brushes, pencils, tubes, and jars is a masterpiece of organization. Natalie's printmaking area, one flight up, resides in the front section of their bedroom. Because-she works more often at school, working at

Opposite: A garden of make-believe flowers in a trio of artful vases blooms on a low table in the front parlor, surrounded by piles of books, toys, and a bowl of delicious knick-knacks. Top: Natalie and son Hoot decked out in her furry designs in the sixties. Bottom: Natalie's woven-rug portrait of Pansy Puff Ball and Cool Dude, and a barbershop quartet from South Africa.

home requires an excavation through layers of fabric and clothes that frequently camouflage it. "When I have to work here, I just clear it out."

And when friends arrive for dinner, which they often do—Natalie is a wonderful cook and she and her husband love to entertain—they tend to resist the bit of calm offered by a seat in the front parlor and make their way into the perfect storm of the kitchen. There, surrounded by the 3-D patchwork of Natalie's things crowded onto the shelves of floor-to-ceiling cupboards, room is made for them around the table. Under the glow of Jon's prized Arts and Crafts lamp and the glitter of Natalie's make-believe parrots, a shiny twirling heart reflects the warmth of flickering candles, their smiling faces, and glasses raised to toast this home sweet home!

Left: The parlor's sofa cozied up with Indian fabrics and pillows beckons to Natalie as a place to rest, which she rarely does since she's always busy with drop-in students, textile projects, or dinner guests. The "kitties in the basket" pillows are digital prints on velvet. The heart-shaped leopard-skin chair caught her eye at a market.
Top: Real fuzzy-wuzzies snuggle together.

This page (clockwise from top left): At the bedroom windows facing the back garden are an encroaching wisteria vine and a rock 'n' roll curtain honoring Elvis; the little pink stool cum coat of arms and roses was brought back from a jaunt to Paris; the headboard of the master bed, which is layered with Mexican spreads, is a mirror Natalie bought at the Portobello antiques market when she was sixteen; the windows seen on the roof look into the other side of the bedroom.
Opposite: *Anything goes atop Natalie's dresser, where a swaying lady from India and a blissful betrothed couple survey a riot of color below, including bags, beads, sashes, and private wear, caught on handy catchall knobs from India.*

I Married Obsession:
The Hoarder's Husband
Speaks Out

Jon has lived with his wife Natalie and her
collected overflow for more than four decades, but he's not counting either the years
or the stuff. Instead, with a kind of if-you-
can't-beat-'em-join-'em attitude, he actually
started using her collected stuff as the subject
of his paintings. A recent series he calls
"Kitchen Kitsch" celebrates the chock-full
landscape of their own kitchen right down
to the last tea strainer, leopard-skin mug, and
yes, even the kitchen sink! Feeling it only
fair to give Jon a chance to rant a little about
what it's like for a man tempered by modern-
ism to live amidst wall-to-wall stuff, he de-
ferred to the cult English writer/novelist Will
Self who, in a piece on one of his "Kitchen
Kitsch" paintings, "actually describes my attitude towards Natalie's hoarding tendency in
a rather perceptive way."

"Jon likes to claim that the vast profusion of
china, glass, figurines, fetish objects, bibelots,
enameled tins, Toby jugs, corn dollies, gonks,
wonks, etc. etc., are all the responsibility of
his wife, Natalie, but the extravagant profusion of small objets in his own studio would
seem to belie this.

"Indeed, I think it is reasonable to sug-
gest that Wealleans—fine and honest artist
that he is—has decided to paint the Kitchen
Kitsch series because he knows how intrinsic
to his own creative process is the concept of
ordered chaos: a seemingly random agglom-
eration of objects that yet contain within
their interrelation the lineaments of the mind
that assembled them."—Will Self

So, is Jon's endorsement of Self's analysis of
his intrinsic need for "ordered chaos" in the
creative process an endorsement of his wife's
disordered chaos? You decide.

*Above: Natalie's stuff is everywhere,
even on her husband's easel.*
*Right: A peek into the second-floor
doorway of Jon's studio framed by
stained glassed parrots on the sides (his)
and a floral rhapsody up above (hers).*

The Tidy Gene: What We Pass On to Our Children

When asked what her sons thought about living with of all the stuff—the cats, birds, and a tangled garden in the back—Natalie pauses, then blurts out, "Well, I ought to ask them! I don't know. One is really tidy and the other one is more like me. One of them doesn't want cats and the other can't live without them. One's rebelled; one hasn't." And who's to say as time goes by that Mr. Tidy might marry someone like his mother and Mr. Messy might fall for Ms. Clean? Will they look back at the lessons of the split housekeeping personalities of their own parents and realize that in the end it was more about the way they lived than the cat hair, the clutter, and what they had to step over?

Though there seems to be no research on the tidy gene, there is an interesting study about what offices and bedrooms reveal about our personalities. Undertaken at the University of Texas, Austin, by psychologist Samuel Gosling, PhD, and his colleagues, and published in the March 2002 issue of APA's *Journal of Personality and Social Psychology*, the study looked for physical cues in the environment, such as tidiness, organization, and decorating style. People with distinctive decorating styles got high marks for openness; those who were neat for conscientiousness. According to Dr. Gosling, "Should you decide to date someone by looking at their bedroom? If openness is important to you, sure. But if extroversion is important, you might want to meet them first."

One of the two bedrooms vacated by Natalie and Jon's sons became a warehouse of sorts for Natalie's overflow. The top of the bureau seen here is a perfect place to lodge a few more cats and a tiny parrot standing next to an image of Natalie's parents. In the mirror is a reflection of one of Jon's "Kitchen Kitsch" paintings.

205

the purposeless room

The no-name repository—a room,
a closet, a cubbyhole, a drawer—
providing refuge and safekeeping for
the not-so-crucial but beloved treasures
of life's overflow.

"The superfluous, a very necessary thing."
—Voltaire

What frivolity to have a room with no purpose. All of the rooms in our homes have assigned duties. We cook in the kitchen; we dine in the dining room; we socialize in the living room; we sleep in the bedroom; and if we are lucky enough to have an attic, a basement, or a garage, we store or park in them life's overflow.

Finding Purpose

For years we had a wayward, identity-less room we dubbed The Purposeless Room. It was a small square room that adjoined the living room, but was not the living room. Its centerpiece was a sturdy wooden table covered with stacks of the red books I collect. A primitive green step-back cupboard displayed my Infant Jesus of Prague statuary collection, a screened pie safe stored oversized books, and a sunny daybed was the favorite napping spot for our dogs and occasionally an overnight guest. It was a catchall kind of room that our family (other than the sleeping dogs) rarely used, and guests passed through quickly not knowing what to do there. It was subject to various ridicule and lots of family debate on the nature of its wasteful life and what sort of useful role it could serve. As time passed our angst subsided and we left the room to its own devices. Perhaps, we

thought, it was not such a bad thing for a room to exist without the burden of a given responsibility, but to simply give pleasure to those who might stray there for a moment to rest and reflect on nothing in particular. And then with the unexpected gift of a baby grand piano (see page 211) that fit perfectly in a corner between two windows, its purposeless life ended. "Ah, and this is the music room!" we exclaim when we take a first-time visitor on a tour. But in our hearts we know this new label is just a defensive maneuver, an empty title, to protect our happy, lazy room from further scrutiny.

Rooms in Transition

Sent on my own to explore the charming three-story house of Natalie Gibson and Jon Wealleans in the Bermondsey section of London (see Case History No. 7, page 189), I came upon a room with a closed door on the second floor. "Nothing's off-limits," Natalie had reassured me, so I slowly pushed it open. Inside raged a storm of hilarious, beautiful, purposeless chaos. A kitty-covered chair—a Natalie textile design—blocked my initial investigation, and then, behind it, under layers of colorful clothes, dresses, sweaters, fabrics, hats, and shoe boxes, I detected the outline of a twin bed. Could this have been the childhood bedroom of one of their two grown sons? "Well, yes," Natalie confirmed, "this had been Hoot's room with Brodie across the hall in what is now Jon's studio." "And," she added, "I probably have more stuff now since they moved out and left more room to fill." So faced with a room bereft of purpose, left undefined by the natural migration of children, these empty-nester parents were left with a positive dilemma: an empty nest to fill. And that they did, leaving most of it intact as a boy's room turned guest room for brave guests and all of that seemingly purposeless stuff that has no place in our lives at the moment, but might at some future time.

Hidden Purpose

Elena Salgueiro yearns for a purposeless corner in her home in Thomery, France (see Case History No. 4, page 105), but bemoans its lack. "I do not stash things when company is coming, for every room in the house remains open and our guests go everywhere—[we have] no hiding place, no attic, no cellar, and no garage since we turned it into a kitchen and more living space for the seven of us."

Every home needs a large or small space with no assigned task or designated duty. Appoint a jar, a bowl, a cubby, a cranny, a chest, a drawer, or a closet to fill with things that at the moment don't have a real purpose, but could at any minute. In that purposeless jar you might store change, especially pennies, as well as buttons and safety pins. Purposeless drawers can carry the burden of the detritus that washes up in the tide of our daily living: a pair of glasses missing a lens; an expired passport or driver's license; a clutch of old holiday cards, postcards, and report cards; children's artwork; sewing kits collected from hotel bathrooms; faded snapshots; belt buck-

les; shells; matchbooks; mate-less earrings; pencil stubs; paperclips; collar stays; broken watches; and batteries. A closet can be the temporary holding area for fans hibernating in winter, ironing boards, extra bedding, coat hangers, suitcases, fabric, wrapping paper, and clothes that seem out of fashion. What would we do without these hideaways? One thought might be to try one of the antidotes suggested under "The Hoarder's Curse" in the following pages.

Previous spread: My garden shed is a limbo for collected things not yet assigned a purpose.
Above: A bowl of purposeless miniatures, including a tiny doll, dust pan, assorted charms, and wayward detritus.

The Hoarder's Curse:
Tips on Letting Go

Being born with the hoarder's instinct to store things, that commonsense rule, "When in doubt, throw it out," just doesn't work for me. If I have doubts, I keep it. Check under my bed and in my closets, my barn, and my pocketbook for evidence. I don't encourage this behavior, or a reckless throw-it-on-the-burn-pile-attitude, either. If you are in my predicament, here are some rules not to live by, but to consider:

In Your Closet:
How many seasons has a piece of clothing hung there without being worn? If at least three, toss it on the pile to give to your favorite thrift shop.

If it is a special one-of-a-kind piece—vintage or otherwise—that you feel is kind of priceless and irreplaceable, create your own archive—a new kind of hope chest, as in "hopefully I'll use this someday." My archival closet (bonus space after my oldest son flew the coop) is deep, so is outfitted with two hanging bars—one in front of the other. I added a third bar up top in front of the upper shelves to hang shirts and jackets. I built in extra shelves to the ceiling to store not only plastic cases of clothes, but photographs, diaries, and journals.

In Your Office:
A friend of mine recently dropped a copy of an article on my desk with a scribbled note in the margin that read, "Carter, I thought you would love this article." I read the headline, "Messy Is the New Neat," from *Time* magazine, January 29, 2007) and smiled, and

then it disappeared in a pile marked "save." Recently I reviewed that avalanche of stuff I couldn't throw away, and just in time for the writing of this book it reappeared. Which is one of the points the author, Jeremy Caplan, makes about filing things too often and too far from hand: "Those with messy desks often stumble upon serendipitous connections between disparate documents." We pack rats love validation.

Look Before You Leap!:
A year ago, getting ready for our older son's wedding and deciding to use the top of our barn for part of the festivities, I feverishly started to sort through my stored collections of junk. I considered having a large tag sale, but imagining the pain of pricing each article, advertising it, and ending up with half of what I started with (maybe) I listened to that little anti-junk angel on my shoulder who whispered, "Burn it, Baby, burn it!" And I did, resulting in a cleaned up barn along with some lingering regrets.

The moral of this story? A ticking clock can deafen wise thinking, or when the clock's ticking you may not be able to hear yourself think. The ideal solution is, of course, to beat the clock by planning ahead, but since real life is rarely ideal, we sometimes have to make decisions under pressure and only in the long run realize our folly.

Purge the Purposeless—Have a Yard Sale:
Though I am constantly planning a mega-yard sale, it hasn't happened yet. Your own tag sale is a great way to unload old clothes,

When we moved a baby grand piano into the front parlor, once dubbed "the purposeless room," it became the music room and its purposeless life was over.

furniture, toys, and all those things that you're constantly tripping over in your garage or attic, the lost-soul kind of stuff that that fills your purposeless drawers and closets. Plus it can be lots of fun to do it with a friend or neighbors or take part in a large one in your community.

Some of the towns in our area publicize special weekends for the whole community to open their garages. Check your local chamber of commerce to take advantage of these events.

My Mother's Holiday Lottery:

Pity my poor mother who has for years allowed her nine children to fill up her beautiful old barn with the souvenirs and leftovers of our individual and collective journeys, habitats, exploits, and enterprises. Being a bit of a hoarder herself (she was the one who taught us!) she is not blameless in the inventory that has taken over every nook and cranny. Ten Christmases ago, she decided it was time to give unto others—us! On Christmas morning we each drew a number out of a hat and took turns seeking out our sort-of-vintage gift from our own curiosity shop—the barn.

We each chose some treasure that had belonged to another sibling or to our mother—an old painted cupboard, a box of mismatched china, a brass chandelier, a slightly crippled armchair, a set of sagging windows, peeling shutters. We tagged our choices and then asked permission to pick them up later (and never did). Poor Mother, her generosity failed!

Good Will:

It can take some work, but donating your overflow—clothes, furniture, even an old car—can really help others, make you feel good, and even be a tax advantage. Goodwill and The Salvation Army are just two giants out of many organizations that would love to take your castoffs (you can find others on the Internet). Depending on where you live and what you have to give, they'll even come to your door and pick up your stuff.

A Few Donation Dos and Don'ts from The Salvation Army:

● Do test all electrical and battery-operated equipment to make sure it's still working prior to donation.

● Do include all manuals, if available.

● Do include all pieces and/or parts.

● Do wash or dry clean any clothing prior to donation.

● Do call ahead of time if dropping items off at a center or store.

● Do bring an itemized list of your donation and ask for a receipt.

● Do not donate broken or soiled items.

● Do not leave items outside a collection box or center.

● Do not donate items that have been recalled, banned, or which otherwise do not meet current safety standards.

Here I am happily surrounded by a truckload of booty from other people's yard sales, but I just can't seem to get plans for my own off the ground. Someday!

Organizing principles

Disorganization is not necessarily a disease or a character flaw. Often a life unorganized can be circumstantial: (a) You live in an apartment or small house without much space; (b) you live in a house designed by an architect who forgot the closets; (c) you were born that way; (d) you are the oldest of nine; (e) you like disorganization. Whatever the reason (or the excuse) even those who seem the most disorganized usually have a few secret weapons to keep them on track. Here are a few drawn from the case histories in this book.

Get Storage with Lots of Drawers:
That's Natalie Gibson's (Case History No. 7, page 189) suggestion. "I love things that have lots of drawers. I always think they're going to sort my life out, but they never do." The one tall skinny bureau in her bedroom (with twenty-seven drawers) is full of her "treasures" inventoried as "jewelry and sewing things, bits of stuff from India, wonderful ribbons, sequins and things like that." She also loves all the little knobs to hang more treasures on, like her colorful bags brought back from India (seen opposite at bottom right).

Another Vote for Lots of Drawers:
A seven-foot-high green cupboard with twelve drawers and several healthy nooks for books and paintings has recently unburdened the one poor dresser my husband and I have shared in our city bedroom for years. The drawers are perfect little pockets for underwear, T-shirts, scarves, belts, caps, socks, leggings, and sweats. Behind the lower door are shelves for stacks of jeans and utility pants that used to live a secret life piled up on the floor shielded by the faded floral heft of an overstuffed armchair (seen opposite at top left).

Go to the Flea Market and Find Something Big and Unique:
Luckily Nathalie Lété (Case History No. 2, page 61) lives a tram ride away from one of the best flea markets in France, the place that created them. When I visited her Ivry studio outside of Paris, she took me to explore her favorite *brocantes* set up along the streets of Porte de Vitry on Sundays. Most of the time she is looking for old toys and the things that inspire her naive creations, but sometimes she comes upon something that can help organize the creative bric-a-brac of her life's work. Stretching almost twenty-four feet along the wall just inside the entrance to her studio is a heavy metal cabinet salvaged from EDF, the French electricity company. Each of the eight five-foot-high units, resembling a lineup of hard-core lockers, stores different fanciful provisions like her collection of fabric odds and ends stacked by themes and color, seen opposite at bottom left.

Put a Mover's Shelf to Permanent Use:
When I switched offices recently, I was totally stumped for an efficient way to move the tons of books I had accumulated over a seventeenyear stay. Surveying the problem, my moving pros rolled in a simple yet ingenious mobile plywood shelf unit (seen opposite at top right). I crammed the five shelves with a good supply of book booty and parked it temporarily in my new office. A few weeks later it was still there. I decided that a

Clockwise from above: My tall green cupboard of drawers; a mover's shelf of books has a permanent place in my office; a twenty-seven-drawer wonder in Natalie Gibson's bedroom provides internal and external storage; Nathalie Lété's flea market find, a utility cabinet from the French electric company, now stores fabric odds and ends.

Clockwise from top left: A scrap-book wall in Pamela Bell's bedroom filled up with her children's heartfelt messages; Elena Salgueiro's "swan song" box stores bonus finds from old books; extra seating and extra storage provided by Pamela Bell's Moroc-can poufs; a camouflage cupboard for Oberto Gili's TV and CD collection.

bookshelf I could push around provided great flexibility in reconfiguring my workspace at a moment's notice. Until another big book-moving job comes along, it looks like I'm safe. In the meantime, I have plans to have a skateboard designer friend create one I can have for keeps.

Organize Your Inspiration with Living Wallpaper—Scrapbook Walls:

For a family of visual learners, Pamela Bell has seen to it that she and her children have plenty of places to save any and all scraps of things that inspire them—torn-out pages from magazines, programs from exhibits and performances, sketches, swatches, pieces of ribbon, party favors, invitations, postcards, and letters. All go up on the oversized bulletin boards scattered throughout their home (seen opposite at top left). Some are personal projects created in the privacy of their bedroom and one is for all to share in their community workspace. Though scrapbooks are a fine way of collecting personal memorabilia, a scrapbook wall is an even better way of saving, sharing, and organizing random bits of inspiration, as well as displaying reminders of doctors' appointments, parties, weddings, teachers' meetings, etc. Though plenty are available assembled, to customize a space, go to a Home Depot kind of place, and DIY!

Oberto Gili's TV Sleight-of-Hand:

Oberto doesn't mince words, particularly when it comes to his TV. "I hate it!," he says. But because he feels, like many of us, that having one in the house is essential ("I just don't want to see it!"), he has hidden it in a tall blue-and-yellow-painted armoire from an antiques shop near his other home in Italy (seen opposite at bottom left). Standing as it does in a corner of his kitchen, some unsuspecting guest might open its door seeking a wine glass or dishes to set the table, and instead find the hidden components of Oberto's techy life—not only the TV, but a CD player and very ordered stacks of his favorite music.

Elena Salgueiro's "Swan Song" Box:

Elena saves and savors the bonus bits and pieces she often finds tucked inside old books—a dictation dating back to World War I, metro tickets from World War II, newspaper articles from 1903, votive cards, sixties-era chewing gum wrappers, a calendar from 1897—by storing them in another found treasure—her weathered "swan song" box (seen opposite at top right). Ornamental boxes, vintage lunch boxes, cigar boxes, and old metal strong boxes are a handy way to keep loved loose ends under control and out in the open so you can enjoy them at a moment's notice.

Chic Ingenuity:

When Pamela Bell returned home with a bunch of golden leathery poufs (seen opposite at bottom right), picked up for a song at the souk in Morocco, the idea was to spread them around the house for extra seating. When it came time to stuff them her son Will came up with the idea of using their sleeping bags as filler. Who would ever guess these chic little seaters are clever storage units as well?

living with fashion

case history no. 8 **daniela kamiliotis**

How an artist and fashion designer seeking freedom of expression left Romania and everything she loved (including her parents) and found it (and a soul mate) in New York City and eventually in a light-filled studio attached to a cottage in rural Connecticut.

daniela

Born in: Bucharest, Romania
Family: her husband Thanos and
many friends
Home and studio: Bethel, Connecticut
Lived there: twenty years
Description: a studio, with concrete paint-
spattered floors and wrap-around
windows and, a house built in the thirties
Challenge: how not to become buried in your
own creative space and forget about the rest of
your life (especially your husband
and friends)
Solution: always searching for balance
Why do people feel at home in your house?
Because it's so casual and like a gallery with
lots to look at and discover
**Most important thing to make friends feel
comfortable?** Sitting down at a beautiful table
to share good food, drink, and conversation
Words to live by: "Wherever I live is my
studio!" (make every room a place to create)

*Previous spread: Posing outside her
Connecticut studio, a trio of Daniela
Kamiliotis's artful characters expressed
on her favorite canvas—the dress form.
This page (clockwise from top): The
artist snaps pictures of her costumed
ensemble; a mélange of artificial
flowers, vintage jewelry, and military
medals; Daniela's paint-spattered
personalized chair.
Opposite: Telltale signs of the creative
process surround a smock-draped
easel and an unfinished portrait in
Daniela's studio with wrap-around
windows.*

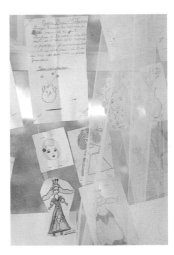

"Wherever I live is my studio," declares an exotic-looking woman in a long, paint-spattered smock with tanned bare feet sticking out at the bottom and a cap of feathery white blond hair framing the kind of expressive face an artist would want to paint—except she is the artist Daniela Kamiliotis. Whether she's working on designing a women's collection with Ralph Lauren in her draped and cluttered office in New York City, painting in her living room across town, or at work on a huge canvas in her real artist's space in rural Connecticut, each is her studio. She thinks of a studio as "a real living space," but quickly adds that "any room—a bedroom, a living room—is a living space as well." An artist's studio is a place of work that quickly fills up with the tools required for the project at hand. In Daniela's case that could be clay, tubes of paint, rollers, bolts of fabric, pots of dye, pencils, sculpting tools, potter's wheels, slab rollers—anything she might need for the many mediums she works in. She vows her studio is not a room she decorates to make a creative statement, but "alive with works in progress." Its look changes depending upon the project. Today buckets of blue dye and a long trail of gauzy blue fabric hanging from one of her twenty-foot windowed walls (looking like a raggy ballgown for an artist princess, the kind she drew when she was a little girl) set a romantic mood of pastel sky and watery hues.

"You can't worry about how neat everything is around you when you are working on a project."

—Daniela

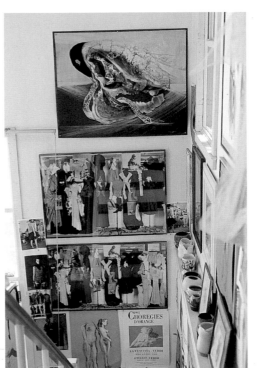

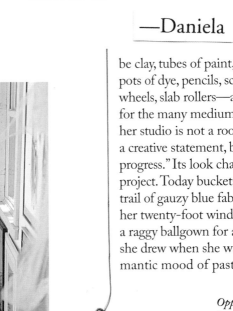

Opposite: The "stairway to heaven" is how Daniela describes the steps that link her upstairs living space with her downstairs studio.
Top: A tulle-draped window displays a collection of childhood drawings.
Bottom: A scrapbook wall of fashion inspiration, and above it an early painting entitled "Metamorphosis." Along the ledge are first trials of her clay vases.

The studio's permanent collection includes a self-portrait painted as if through ashes the day after 9/11, and next to it (as if to connect the present to the past), her portrait of her father done in Romania in 1978. The haphazard lineup of empty frames, sketches, and old photographs sits quite reverently on an old church bench. The fluffy white cutout flowers romanticize a dangling light bulb.

She started her artistic journey the day she was born to Ileana and Andrei Codarcea, well-known Romanian actors in Bucharest. They like the rest of her family believed that being an artist was the most incredible role in society—a talent to be respected and developed. At age five, displaying a natural talent for drawing—"mostly princesses and dresses," she admits—her grandmother took her to study at a real center for the arts. Surrounded by students five times her age and older, she started painting in oil. From then until she finished her six years at Bucharest's Academy of Art, she did nothing else. Having grown up on the sets of the many stages and film locations where her parents performed, it is not surprising she chose to get a master's degree in costume and set design. Not only was she looking for a way to put her art to work, but in her heart she knew that her personality was not suited to the solitary life of a painter. She wanted "to be part of a team and build together." For six years those teams were made up of a slew of the top theater and film directors, and set and costume designers from Bucharest to Moscow, London, and New York. Though her life was productive—thirty theater productions and six films from the time she graduated—living under a communist regime ultimately shaped her decision to seek political asylum in Greece at age thirty. Simply put, she felt "an artist needs to be totally free." She left Bucharest with ninety dollars and a suitcase full of drawings. She remembers the faces of her mother, father, and grandmother as her train pulled away, wondering whether she would ever see them again. After arriving in Greece she went directly to the Red Cross and applied for asylum, which she was granted immediately. She chose to live in the United States, in New York City, having interned there once for famed costume designer Theoni Aldredge. During the eight months she waited for her working papers, she made money selling her work in three exhibitions and creating accessories for a very successful Greek fashion designer. She spoke to her parents daily, but when she tried to bring her eighty-year-old grandmother over for a visit, her visa was denied. (She died soon after that; in Daniela's mind this was the ultimate sacrifice and heartbreak in her quest for freedom.)

It had been five years since her internship in New York, but she had many contacts. One was a young man from Greece who worked in the fashion business. She got in touch with him to seek career advice, but by the time they met she had already looked up Aldredge, who offered her a job on the spot. The Greek man's name was Thanos Kamiliotis; they were married a year later. Looking back over their twenty-two years she is quite clear, "I knew immediately he was the one."

Five years later her parents were able to leave Romania. When they decided to move to New York, Thanos purchased a charming old house outside of the city where they could live and he and Daniela could visit on the weekends. It became the house of her childhood, filled not only with the love of her parents but with all the mementos they carried with them from Romania, including all

Opposite: In preparation for a new exhibition, using her forms as both sculpture and painting inspiration, an empty canvas awaits.
Left: Daniela at twenty-three, creating a costume on a form in Romania.

227

her little childhood drawings. If this was not enough, attached to the house was a wonderful studio built by a former resident, a photographer, where Daniela could take up her paintbrushes again and continue the journey that her parents and grandmother had inspired so many years before.

Daniela's studio is her private world, always changing based on the theme of her present work, with the exception of the personal things that sustain her memories: costumed images of her mother and father at work in the theater, a large portrait of her father that she painted in 1978 (he passed away seven years ago followed a year later by her mother), a self-portrait she did the day after 9/11, a vintage cash register storing a different kind of currency, a treasured collection of more family photos, and last but not least, a nest of her childhood drawings caught in layers of romantic tulle tacked to a window. Besides the de rigueur easels and worktables overflowing with tubes of pigment, and canvases in different stages of completion, there is a unique legion of muslin-covered forms in the studio. From her early days as a student of costume design, she has lived with and worked on forms. "They're my canvas," she states. Equally, they are a natural part of the last fourteen years of her weekday professional life with Ralph Lauren—a sort of artist-in-residence/dream maker/designer and now a senior vice president of his women's collection. They are the "characters" for a design theme she may be developing or a stand-in for a nude she is painting. They roll around easily on the studio's paint-spattered concrete floor.

Above: Everything's a canvas in Daniela's world, including a pair of summer pants exhibiting a painted tale of the high seas worthy of Robert Louis Stevenson.
Opposite: A photo collage of Daniela's family spanning many generations is creatively preserved on a board smeared with thick white paint and gesso.

In Daniela's world, a worktable filled with the disarray and tangle of the artistic tools of her craft becomes a beautiful still life in its own right.

Daniela's upstairs/downstairs worlds are connected by a staircase that runs against a wall on one side, filled like a gallery with sketches ("none took more than ten minutes") and a banister that opens to the studio itself. Thanos is the master of organizing their upstairs life—the kitchen, the living room, a comfortable TV niche (his), the bedrooms, a dining room that looks out on a large deck with a grill where they cook and entertain during the warmer months. And when friends are there, Daniela climbs the stairs and moves into her other creative lair: the kitchen. She loves to cook and believes sharing a meal at a creatively set table is the best way to make friends feel comfortable, to spur conversation, and to her way of thinking, "love each other!" The special touch of her creativity floats up the studio stairs behind her. "I am not interested in seeing walls and floors," she says, which is why most are covered with her art, calligraphy, or stenciling.

Where is she most comfortable? "Every time I arrive at the house, I go straight down to the studio; I don't go to the kitchen or the bedroom. I think about what I am going to do for the weekend, and I prepare a project. Then after everything is set up, I go upstairs to my other heaven and have a glass of wine with Thanos."

Opposite: The sun pours in turning a sheer blouse into a see-through scrim for sketches, a costumed form, and a rack of accessories on Daniela's magical set.
Top: Paintbrush bristles display a picture of a couple of mad hatters— me and Daniela.
Bottom: The pristine exterior of Daniela's studio belies the creative chaos just inside the door.

the unmade bed

The seductive bower of lovers, and
the nest of moms and dads, babies,
children, storybooks, favorite blankets,
toys, and the warmth of furry pets.
A cozy retreat as well as the cradle of
daydreams and imagination.

Make Your Bed

Since we were children it has been ingrained in us to make our beds! Don't you hear that army of mothers, especially your own, roaring out in unison, "Don't forget to make your bed!" My sons heard it from me, and their children one day will hear it from them or from their wives, and to this day I still hear it, and I obey. Not first thing, though, since I share my bed with my husband Howard, who follows me to the kitchen a little later, after I've walked the dog, made the coffee, and picked up the newspaper. But after that, even before I brush my teeth, shower, or start to dress for work, I go to it. Every morning it's the same, circling the perimeter of the bed to pick up the things abandoned to the floor when sleep curtails those last conscious acts of the day: *The Old Curiosity Shop* on my side; a slightly crumpled *New Yorker* and *Sports Illustrated* on Howard's. There's our dog's bed, too, a big, plump denim-covered pup mattress planted on the left side of the bed—my territory, and the side most directly in the line of fresh air from three big windows open year-round, except on the hottest nights when the detested air conditioner goes on or on the coldest nights when a big whoosh sends a delicate lace of snowflakes onto our protective pile of cozy flannels. After bed patrol, I pull the top sheet and duvet to the foot of the bed, smooth out the bottom sheet, puff up a half-dozen pillows, then tuck dangling sheets in place and retrieve several old decorative pillows (flung nightly to a nearby chaise) and place them on top of our fluffy pillow peaks. At about this time, which is no more than five minutes, Howard will arrive and plunk himself down on our perfectly made bed. I bellow!

Nest

Our bed has been our nest and that of our children and dogs for thirty-six years. Since my father helped construct its headboard (seen below) out of a wide weathered floorboard secured by two skinny trapstakes—driftwood relics of the pine trees supporting fishing nets in the waters near my childhood home in Virginia—it has not changed shape nor appearance nor even location. It's a bit of a sham bed, really, since the box springs and mattress are supported by a metal frame on wheels that allows us to move it easily away from the attached headboard when floors need polishing or walls repainting. The only alteration has been the frame's height, raised about a foot some years ago with the help of those handy plastic cones created for storage-bereft people like me who are in desperate need of hiding places for bins of life's overflow.

Elena Salgueiro (Case History No. 4, page 105) is always searching for an old mantel to use for her bed's headboard, but so far she has not found the suitable one. Until then, she is content to live with the ornately carved metal mantel that is a little small for the mattress. She doesn't care since it's only a pretender propped against the wall. She likes the deep rusty red color of it, which matches the bed's flowered coverlet (seen on page 118).

Leave it to Natalie Gibson (Case History No. 7, page 189) to have created the perfect sleeping nest at the very top of the tall, skinny house that has been her home with her husband for over forty years. At its head, reflecting the warm glow of the pink walls that surround it and the sunlight pouring in from

a bank of windows trimmed in her favorite Moroccan blue paint, is a framed mirror that she describes as "not particularly special," but has been with her since she was sixteen. She foraged it from the Portobello Market (see page 200) and eventually stowed it at the head of the bed out of sheer convenience. "There was no other place to put it." A mix of Mexican serapes layers the bed, which usually is a nest for one or two of their eight cats. Her husband would prefer it otherwise, she thinks, but lacking a bedroom door there is no way to keep them out.

Refuge

Beds are our refuge from fatigue, sickness, boredom, company, and oftentimes, life's little unexpected embarrassments. We retreat to them for healing with comfort food; a steamy cup of tea, a nourishing bowl of chicken soup, a dish of frosty ice cream or sherbet. As a child I remember orange popsicles for a sore throat and, when appetite failed, a bowl of bananas smushed by my mother with a touch of milk and sugar added. In Elena Salgueiro's world, a little antique bed, "a couchette," (seen on page 113) tucked into a peaceful corner of their downstairs living room is the place her children retreat when they are sick or, as Elena puts it, "melancholically tuned." "They watch the green of the garden through the milky. To be in bed when the sun is high, when the rest of the world is wide awake at school or work is a guiltless treat.

Not long after we were married I arranged for my husband Howard to have his hair cut by a famed hairdresser. I retreated undercover

Previous spread: A handcrafted bed of driftwood posts entwined with blooming grapevines that dangle above a rumpled cotton spread creates a romantic mood.
Opposite: Beds are nests for families, storybook reading, and favorite toys.
Left: Beds are the refuge of feverish children.

237

with him for two days after his beautiful locks were shorn to a humiliating length. Oh, the comfort of burying oneself under the protective fluff of one's favorite pillow and downy quilt!

Playpen

Once children are born, a bed can quickly be transformed into a substitute cradle or playpen. How many nights have we fallen asleep with our tiny babies tucked between us protected by a pillowed fortress lest we roll the wrong way or wakened suddenly in the middle of the night to find a small pajama-ed person with tear-stained face staring through the darkness seeking the security of our nightmare-proof bed? Is there a better place to be read a story, to build a tent, to snuggle with favorite blankets, teddies and toys?

Studio

I have always loved the image of a pajama-clad Henri Matisse sitting in his bed cutting out what looked like paper dolls—the famous cutouts of his later life. Turning his bed into his studio was not his preference, but his infirmities were not going to stop the progress of his creativity. He once wrote to a friend, "You see I am obliged to remain often in bed because of the state of my health. I have made a little garden all around me where I can walk . . . there are leaves, fruits, a bird." That image came to mind when I walked into the bedroom my son Carter was staying in one Christmas at my family's home in Virginia. Dangling over the bed were his drying negatives pinned onto a makeshift clothesline. His cozy bedroom and small rumpled bed had become his temporary studio.

My son Carter's makeshift bedroom studio strung with a clothesline for drying negatives. The book on the bed was a gift from the photographer Bruce Weber, whom he once assisted.

The Search for the Perfect Bed

When my son Carter and his wife Kasia first moved into their new apartment, they agreed to bring nothing with them except very personal things: photographs, paintings, clothes, and books. What was left behind—sofas, tables, chairs, beds—was sold, given away, or hauled up to our barn in the country. For months they slept on an air mattress on the floor while they searched for the perfect bed. They had agreed it should be wooden and not too shiny. After many were rejected, they found it, not wooden, but iron, as they passed a yard full of them in front of an old brass and iron bed outpost in upstate New York. They had it refurbished and customized to fit a queen-size mattress; when it was finally delivered, they felt their home had found its heart.

They did not spend as much time searching for the perfect mattress. When it arrived they were sorely distressed to find that the combined height of the mattress and the supporting box spring (which was not a box spring but a steel grid foundation) was so high that after placing their pillows on top, they could hardly see the ornate beauty of the bed they had spent so much time searching for. The moral of the story? Make key measurements before committing to a new mattress for an old bed. Or in Kasia and Carter's case, trade your new too-high box spring for your parents' older, narrower one.

My son and daughter-in-law's perfect bed imperfectly strewn with cream-colored sheets and pillows and personalized with a monogrammed blanket thrown over its ornamental iron footboard. Over the headboard is their collection of weathered painted frames awaiting the perfect pictures.

Unmade

I have made up my bed close to twenty-two thousand times! It's part of a ritual that contributes a continuity and shape to my days. It's a simple feat, but extremely satisfying. As I leave our room in the morning I sometimes glance back and see the blue tufted balls of our summer bedspread lined up correctly; two stacks of pillows piled high in soft white cases; the multicolored chain of construction paper drifting above them with the little sugar heart I bought years ago in a shop in Milan hanging in its center; and a photograph of my mother and father sitting in our family kitchen on a Christmas morning a decade ago stuck in a primitively carved green wooden frame leaning on the left side of the headboard right above where I sleep. As much as I love this vision of my perfectly made bed, I am just as in love with the bed unmade—pillows squished and shoved from sleepy heads, covers pushed back, sheets rippled like desert sands, a book left behind for the smell of coffee, a child's cry, a dog to be walked, a car to be moved, a meeting to make—in other words, a new day. The unmade bed is the romantic fingerprint of a night that has passed for a young couple for whom sharing a bed is a new wonder, for an old couple who has slept through many a storm and cling to each other out of comfort and familiarity, for a boy and his dog, for two little sisters and their dolls.

An unmade bed, though pretty in pictures, is a little like dishes left in the sink overnight. Just as we would prefer to have clean dishes in the morning, so too would we prefer to climb into a perfectly made bed at the end of the day.

243

living with junk

case history no. 9 mary randolph carter

How a lover of all things old (junk to others) filled an old house in the country with her many collections while squeezing in plenty of comfort for her friends and family.

Carter

Born in: Virginia
Family: my husband
Howard, my sons Sam and Carter, and my
daughter-in-law Kasia
Homes: Upper East Side, New York City, and
Dutchess County, New York
Lived there: thirty-five years (apartment);
twenty-three years (farm)
Description: an old apartment (circa 1938);
an old white clapboard
farmhouse (circa 1800)
Challenges: finding a comfortable chair for
my husband and a place for all my junk
Solution: still searching
Inspiration: the character of old things
Words to live by: Please, Lord, let me
find it here!
A Perfect House? Never, never, never

*Previous spread: My favorite junking
gear hooked on the back of our kitchen
door with old faithful work boots
standing by.*
*This page (clockwise from top):
Standing proud with my junker's
catch of the day; a wooden replica of
the junker's transport—a pickup truck;
guarding the front door is a vintage
flag and an owl decoy.*
*Opposite: Outside the kitchen door is
a little altar to wildlife: birds, berries,
dried flowers, and garden tools.*

For the best view of Elm Glen Farm against a backdrop of autumnal splendor, plop down in one of the trio of old rusty garden chairs in the shadow of our birch tree flagpole and the flapping colors of our country.

my refrigerator kind of tells my story. After we bought it, the glossy white thing stood out like a sore thumb amidst the colorful clutter of the rest of the room. I had no choice but to camouflage it. I started with some extra rolls of black and white checkered contact paper, but when my husband said it looked like something left over from a NASCAR event, I kept going and turned it into a bulletin board taped from top to bottom with Polaroids of visiting family and friends. It fits in perfectly now and everyone loves it, particularly me.

It's obvious I have a real aversion to anything new. It wasn't always this way; it happened over time. Factor in growing up in a seventeenth-century house in Virginia, that region's reverence for the past, and most of all, my mother and father's predilection for all things old—houses, hardware, textiles, and furnishings—and, well, new stuff just didn't have a chance. When I moved into my first apartment, a fifth-floor walk-up on Manhattan's Upper East Side, I hauled up an old blue rocking chair, a drop-leaf table (missing one of the leaves), a couple of aged milking stools, a few faded quilts and coverlets, some primitive paintings, and favorite books and family photographs to re-create some of the well-worn comforts of the home I had left behind. Each time I climbed up those stairs, unlocked all the locks, and opened the door I felt its welcoming spirit all over again. I created a cozy nest that visiting friends described as "different," quirky, comfy and "very Carter,"

which was the nicest compliment of all. It was a place that told my story, and to this day, the homes I love the most (including those that I've created since then with my husband of almost forty years and our two sons, pets, friends, and family) are those that do just that—share the personal history of the people who live there.

In building a case for living life with the things that you love and not worrying too much about everything being perfect, my particular case history is the case for junk! Many of those old pieces that warmed up my first apartment are with me and my husband still in our apartment in New York City and in our oldish (circa 1800) farmhouse in upstate New York.

Since new stuff was out of the question, except for our mattress and possibly the sleep sofa (a wedding present happily accepted from Howard's mother and father), and his glass and chrome coffee table that was quickly dispatched to one of my brothers, the collection of old things grew, sometimes out of necessity (furnishing a larger apartment and a house in the country), but often out of my passion for hunting down slightly aged and patina-ed treasures at auctions, flea markets, yard sales, garage sales, and side-of-the-road giveaways. I was a bit of a snob when I began this journey, seeking out mostly primitive art, textiles, and painted furniture in legitimate antiques shops and shows. As time went by (a decade at least) and those special things became harder to find and harder on the pocketbook, I gave it up. The thrill of the hunt was gone, and so was the fun. Until that fateful

Opposite: Polaroids of family and friends, a magnetic flag, and Henri Rousseau provide camouflage for the front of our plain-Jane refrigerator, which is wallpapered in black-and-white-checked contact paper.
Left: A portrait of Elm Glen Farm painted by the former owner in the fifties.

251

A pink electric clock ticks off the seconds in our country kitchen. It is surrounded by old-fashioned but very useful crockery, silver-ware, salt and pepper shakers, a tin butter keeper (for kitchen matches), a line of orange ovenproof pots, and just-baked breads and pie straight from (somebody else's) oven.

Top: A mishmash of one-of-a-kind pillows.
Bottom: A seaworthy shelf encrusted with barnacle bits hosts shell life galore.
Opposite: Our cozy farm office warmed up with wall-to-wall thrift shop landscapes mirroring the seasons of life in the country. The red wooden telephone on a shelf filled with mostly vintage cookbooks is my romantic answer to a cell phone.

day I pulled my pickup up to a rummage shop I had passed a thousand times near our house in the country. In its prime, it had been a muffler shop distinguished by a gigantic spider on the roof made out of worn-out tail pipes. The spider had often caught my eye, as well as the lineup of people waiting to enter on Sunday mornings (the only day it was open, from ten to three o'clock), but what could I possibly find among the abandoned goods of others decamped in a shop decorated with shiny hubcaps outside and a little hand-painted exhortation in the window, "Bless this Mess." What drove me there on that particular morning almost two decades ago was more than likely an innate stirring deep inside to rejoin that curiously insatiable desire for the hunt. I entered with low expectations and somewhere between the second and third aisles crowded with other people's leftover pots and pans, tablecloths, knickknacks, scissors, thimbles, art school canvases, craft projects, and humble furnishings, I experienced a junker's conversion. By the time I walked out, triumphantly weighed down with arms full of booty, I was no longer that frustrated collector but a born-again soldier of my own fortune, setting out on a new junker's hunt for the worth of the worthless. I left with a little statue of the Infant Jesus of Prague (head glued on) for a dollar, a trio of original landscapes for four, a bunch of fifty-cent wooden picture frames, a working lamp made out of a hand-painted bottle for five dollars, and so much more, including a smile on my face, for under twenty-five dollars! The

In our blooming bedroom flowers sprout from paintings, an old hand-painted green head-board, a faded floral lampshade, a romantic rose-covered chair, an enamel mirror dangling from the dresser stand, the flowered chenille coverlet and, finally, a pillow embroidered with the message "Some Daisies Will Tell."

beauty of junk, I realized that day, is truly in the eye of the beholder. I began to realign my collector's values to coincide with a hunt for things that give me personal pleasure rather than some fancy provenance. I've never looked back. I hunt for the things that are valuable to me (nobody else): a rusty tin box, a paint-spattered chair, a child's tattered scrapbook, a well-used prayer book, paint-by-number masterpieces, patchwork blankets, watering cans, a stringless violin. I find a new home for them on a crowded mantle, a bedroom wall, a kitchen counter, or a desk already overflowing with their orphaned cousins. Together they create a funny kind of visual harmony that is music to my ears and eyes.

"Never stop to think,

Do I have a place for this?"

—Carter

When we first moved into Elm Glen Farm, the charming old white clapboard/green shuttered farmhouse that we purchased in 1988, I wasn't sure how to mingle my rustic collections and junkshop paintings with the rather prim flowered wallpaper and white organza curtains left behind by the former owners. Once the wallpaper was replaced with fresh white paint and the frilly curtains with more stoic ones cut from vintage wool or cotton blankets, the house became the perfect foil to my very disparate collections. After two dozen years, and a lot more junking, there's little space left to add even one more painting. Luckily there are alternate spaces—an old two-story carriage house and a barn with

Opposite: A white wall for me is like a blank canvas to fill with a pastiche of mismatched elements.
Top: Prepared for a cold winter's night, extra blankets keep watch at the foot of the guest room's iron bed.
Bottom: Flowers bloom inside and out our kitchen window flanked by old green shutters and a hand-painted flowerbox that is home to a solitary black wooden crow.

259

a huge loft. The former is now the address of my new clutter-free studio (see page 265 for the flabbergasting story of how I reigned in hundreds of books and lots of mementos), and the barn? Well, that's more like Dorian Gray's picture, filled like a disheveled attic with all the clutter that once lived in my spiffed-up new space!

When our two sons were little, riding through the countryside with Daddy at the wheel and Mom beside him, one of them would spot a yard sale sign on the horizon and quickly gesture to the other to cover my eyes, and then with great anxiety commanded their father to "step on the gas!" I'd play along, of course, even though I'd spotted that sign way before they did, knowing that just around the corner there'd be another one and this time I'd get my way because "I brake for junk."

Now these sons are grown and both have homes they're filling with their own kinds of treasured junk (not in their eyes, of course). And guess who they're calling to take them on the hunt? Their junk-loving mom, of course!

To liven up the kitchen I painted the not-so-old floorboards white and smeared blue paint around the base of the table and a different shade around the door trim. I was attempting to match the perfectly faded color of the weathered shutters.

clutter free

The joyful contradiction of a Zen-like space that makes room for books, toys, art, personal mementos, and clutter with a liberating built-in order.

have always lived with things underfoot, walls packed with paintings, rooms suffocated with things, so I find myself at a loss to explain my sudden love affair with a big, empty white room. It is a room that has been part of my life for quite a while, but with a different look and feel altogether. Tucked atop our carriage house at Elm Glen Farm it has (for over two decades) been a home to my wayward junk collections, leftovers from our sons' college years and first apartments, a cozy refuge for mice, chipmunks, and hidden up in the cupola, those scary creatures that have haunted me since childhood—bats!

My friends used to laugh when I told them of a time in the future when I would clean out our layered apartment in New York City and distill it down to a few important things: a long plank table, a few stools, some books, a bed, and not much else. After the purchase of our farmhouse, I felt I could stop the pretense of creating that country feeling in an apartment and transfer the rocking chairs, quilts, and samplers to a more authentic environment. And so I did, but somehow the spaces made free by their removal were filled with other things. My vision of living with less was not to happen in our city nest. Instead, provoked by a move to a smaller office at my place of work, I realized I needed to find a home for treasures (mostly books) accumulated and stored in that space for seventeen years. The loft in our carriage house has twenty-five-foot ceilings and in my mind I began to imagine thick wooden shelves covering the inside wall and reaching from the floor to the tip of its beamed ceiling. I imagined a year-round studio that would be a permanent home to the books, journals, souvenirs of photo shoots and travels, and mementos from friends and colleagues that would keep me company. To bring the outside views of woods and sky inside and to fill the space with natural light required the addition of lots of windows—a huge five-by-six-foot window facing north and six square windows around the periphery. Everything was painted white and the new floor was left a natural color. Its centerpiece became a massive seventeen-foot-long-by-six-foot-wide worktable built by a friend to accommodate my large-scale layouts of books and other visual projects. We picked a height that allows me to stand over my work without that backbreaking bending. Once my books and magazines filled the shelves, interrupted by occasional mementos—a red and white autographed basketball, a miniature lighthouse, framed pictures and paintings, an oversized pinecone from Yosemite, toy trucks, patchwork clowns, a twig birdhouse, a band of colorful elves—I decided nothing would be allowed to stray beyond the borders of the shelves, which have organized my clutter like a gallery. Featured are the covers of my favorite books exhibited like pictures leaning against the back wall. Garden books commune with garden bric-a-brac, children's books with vintage toys, David Hockney with Vincent Van Gogh, and Manet with Monet and other impressionist cousins. High above them all on a shelf of their own dwell my favorite girlhood mysteries all solved by that

Previous spread: In my clutter-free studio my six-foot-wide custom worktable provides room for sprawling creativity.
Opposite: Books, magazines, and souvenirs fill a wall of shelves that climbs to the twenty-five-foot peak of what once had been a carriage-house hayloft.

The gallerylike shelves that span the twenty-five-foot wall of my studio are accessed by an old apple-picking ladder shoed in rubber slide-proof booties.

wondrous golden-haired sleuth Nancy Drew. To reach those heights I climb up a gleaming white ladder once used for apple picking. A pair of rubber booties prevents it from slipping or scratching the floor.

So here I am in my clean white studio with the things that I love corralled in a towering wall of shelves. I am quite content (for now) to leave well enough alone, meaning the three other walls are unblemished by my addiction to hang stuff everywhere. Those friends that scoffed at my suggestion that I might inhabit a place like this are amazed, even dumbfounded, when they first see it. They don't understand how I could give up (at least during the time I spend in my studio) all the clutter that has happily haunted every room I have lived or worked in as long as they have known me. And then they turn around and spy my scrapbook wall of shelves and understand that I have not denied myself anything just found a new way to live with it.

Tired of spending my life bending over low tables to work, my new table was built to a little over waist height. The little green tractor behind me is, so far, the only memento I've allowed outside the boundary of the heavily laden shelves on the opposite wall.

afterword

When I started planning this book the thought struck me to go outside of my own home and even my own country to share the home truths of others. I was inspired to do this, in particular, by a young mother of five living in a small village in France. I had never met her, but she had emailed often over the course of seven years after discovering my first book, *American Family Style,* and then my books on junk. Though I had never seen Elena Salgueiro's home or pictures of her and her family, I had a feeling for how they might live. Not long after sharing my book idea with her she responded with this, "I'm beginning to understand that we spend our childhoods hurrying up for the future to leave our imperfect limbo for some perfect Promised Land. And this is right and it has to be so. We leave the places where we were born to create new homes somewhere else. But then, as it comes, we spend the rest of our human seasons rummaging in desperate attempts to re-create this same childhood limbo we had been in such a hurry to leave . . ."

No matter where we live, in a country cottage or a brownstone in the city, in a house that we built ourselves or one built by hands we never knew, we choose a place to call home and create in it a life that suits us and those that we share it with—family members, dogs, cats, and, of course, our extended family and friends. We fill it with memory and dreams, and possibly too many things, but whether cluttered or clean we do our best to be good housekeepers, making our homes the perfect place for living.

Mary Randolph Carter

Elm Glen Farm

acknowledgments

To my mother and father, who taught me that a perfect house is a home full of love. And to my sisters and brothers, who filled it with their joyous tumult.

To my husband Howard, who for four decades has always believed our home was perfectly imperfect, except for the lack of a comfortable chair or sofa, and whose most comfortable place to read is our old wooden bed filled with my books and papers and . . . me.

To our sons Sam and Carter, who over the years have filled our home with baseball cards, bats, gloves, golf clubs, hockey sticks, basketballs, Legos, Smurfs, super-heroes, books, and their creativity and energy, and who never complained that their home was just a little bit different from those of their friends. To this day they relish it and still love to return for family meals, which now include Carter's wonderful wife Kasia.

To my special friends, the case histories of this book, who opened their doors and hearts and shared their perfect living throughout the pages of this imperfect book; Pamela Bell and her children Elenore, Anabel, and Will; Natalie Gibson and Jon Wealleans; Oberto Gili; Daniela and Thanos Kamiliotis; Nathalie Lété; my sister Liza Carter Norton; Geri and Jim Roper and their quartet of spaniels, Dash, Elle, Wylie, and Henry; Elena and Daniel Salgueiro and their children, Ksenia, Alice, Tom, Nella, and just-born Diane!

To my dear friend Marie France Boyer, who told me I could not do this book without including her friend Natalie Gibson and all her cats; she was right. To Penelope Green, whose article in the *New York Times* connected me to Pamela Bell. To Joe Zullo for helping me to finally realize a clutter-free space in my life, and to Josh Paris and Kitty Barenbrier for allowing me to take pictures of their wonderful old houses.

To the supporting image makers of this book: Todd Selby for sharing his pictures of my office from his unique site, theselby.com; to Arthur Elgort for some oldies but goodies; to Pedro Guerrero for his images of the studio and home of Alexander Calder (pages 14, 15, 16–17), to Carl Larsson for his wonderful watercolor portrait of his five children from 1894; and last but not least, a huge hug and special thanks to my son and photographer Carter Berg, who shared dozens of his memorable images of our life at Elm Glen Farm and our sweet dog Charley.

To Ralph Lauren, who wrote the foreword to my first book, *American Family Style*, over two decades ago, and then invited me to join his Polo family. His creative and generous spirit has supported and inspired me ever since.

To my team at Rizzoli: publisher Charles Miers, who upon hearing about the words inscribed on our family doormat, immediately said, "Carter, that is the title of your next book!" and kept encouraging and never looked back; to my perfectly incorrigible, thoughtful, talented, and never-without-a-sense-of-humor editor Ellen Nidy, who mothered this book and her new son Oscar in the very spirit of what it stands for, living fully; to Maria Pia Gramaglia for being the guardian angel of each page; and to Jennifer Pierson, Pam Sommers, and Nicki Clendening for getting my message out into the world.

To my Irish wizard, designer and friend Aoife, who took my dream of the life imperfect and turned it into a living volume that reminds me again of how individual passion and true attention to detail can transform lowly ink and paper into a book that is alive with feeling.

And, finally, to the unknown writer who penned the thought, "A perfectly kept house is the sign of a mis-spent life." And to Dame Rose Macaulay who put it another way, "At the worst, a house unkept cannot be so distressing as a life unlived." Amen. Amen.

(And to Charley, who slept under my feet for almost two years as I wrote this book.)

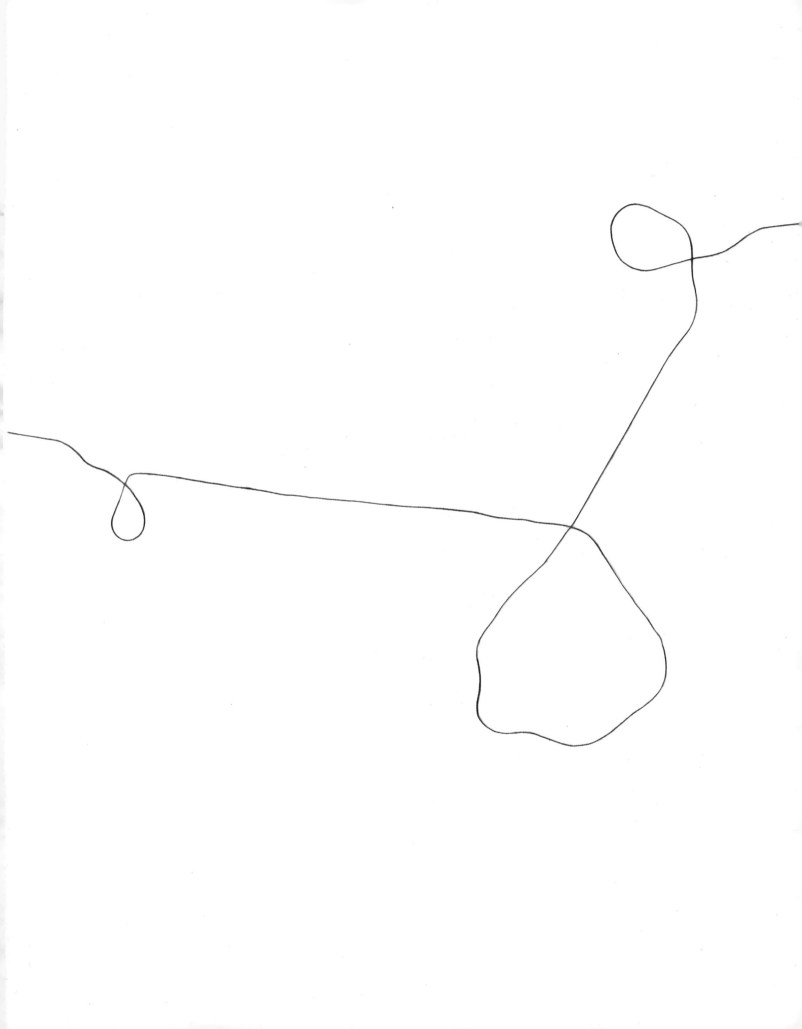